ELLE WILSON

THE
POWER
Shift

FIVE PRINCIPLES THAT WILL CHANGE YOUR LIFE

Copyright © 2018 Elle Wilson

www.ellewilson.com.au

First published in Australia in 2018
by Karen Mc Dermott
www.karenmcdermott.com.au

Edited by: Natasha Gilmour
Cover photo by: Linda Puetter
Cover & Interior Design: Kelsea Gwendoline

All rights reserved. No part of this book may be used or reproduced by any means, graphic, electronic, or mechanical, including photocopying, recording, taping or by any information storage retrieval system without the written permission of the copyright owner except in the case of brief quotations embodied in critical articles and reviews.

The information and concepts contained within this publication are general in nature and should not be treated as a substitute for professional medical advice. The intent is to offer a variety of information to provide a wider range of choices, recognizing that we all have widely diverse circumstances and viewpoints. Any use of information contained in this publication is at the reader's discretion and risk. The contributors, companies, authors and publishers do not assume any responsibility whatsoever under any condition or circumstances. It is recommended that the reader obtain their own independent advice prior to implementing any of the ideas or instructions contained in this book.

National Library of Australia Cataloguing-in-Publication data:
The Power Shift/Elle Wilson
Non Fiction/Self-Help

ISBN: (sc) 978-0-6482497-7-1
ISBN: (e) 978-0-6483037-7-0

Power shifting is a lifetime commitment.

Join me as we together make real one of the greatest accomplishments a human being can aspire to.

Make your life a living testament to truth and let us embrace the joy, the Love and beauty that rises up from within.

Find me at ellewilson.com.au

Love,

Elle Wilson

*This book is dedicated to my loving, patient husband,
my precious children, Yianni and Olivia, my dear stepson Ethan,
and every woman who walks the earth.
May love prevail within you!*

CONTENTS

Foreword	ix
Author's Note	xi
Higher Love	xvii
What it Means	1
A Note on Terms	5
Principle One	13
Principle Two	55
Principle Three	98
Principle Four	113
Principle Five	127
Logos (λόγος)	167

FOREWORD

The marketplace is glutted with how to books with new age advice and with spiritual tomes. One may reasonably question why another, particularly at a time when society suffers an information overload? Indeed, Herbert Simon, the American social scientist, observed, "when there is a wealth of information, there is a poverty of attention."

So why then should you give this book your attention? I can only reply with a personal perspective. This book captured my attention for these three reasons:

One, Elle is not a classic consultant, nor is she a writer looking for a "hot" topic. Elle is living what she is writing. This is not just a book, **it is a life articulated**. The words were written in her actions, before they found expression through her pen.

Two, Elle fundamentally understands that a how-to book which addresses your circumstances will never truly change your outcomes. We are not in control of our circumstances, but we are in control of our responses. The ability to generate **positive energy amidst seemingly negative results** is the key to surviving both failure and success.

Three, the message is **simple but not easy**. We live in a generation of people looking for easy. "Experts" tend to complicate the simple while selling "easy" solutions to the hardest problems. This book is different.

For these three reasons and more this message is both old and new, and thus timely and timeless. It's only value will be determined by you as you choose each moment what to do with its message.

Flint McGlaughlin
Ponte Vedra Beach, FL
2019

AUTHOR'S NOTE

When my brother died, I was thirteen years old and I made my whole life about taking care of others, mainly my father. I externalised my happiness to the extreme and failed dismally. When I was nineteen, I had no inner ground left to live my life from. I had been using the wrong life curriculum for so long, I had forgotten what little I remembered of Love. My responsibility had shifted to try and fix everything. It was my way of dealing with the grief and the lack that I was faced with. Even as a little child, I saw myself as different, as an outsider. I knew too much and yet had forgotten how to be what I knew. I had turned my back on my own inner world and built a false one, where others held the power to my happiness, my safety and my peace. I was living a false life from a very young age. I became lost inside and had forgotten my origin. Lack brought fear and anxiety and I became a testament to these emotions.

However, as dismal as it all sounds, as a young girl I had music and my brothers and sisters to rely on for happier moments. We laughed and played together. My brothers taught me my ABCs, cared for me, and my sisters offered much to look up to. I had in this large family so many beautiful moments. The most important was when I made my father proud, I became addicted to this and when my brother passed, my father needed caring for. He became my responsibility instead of leaning into Love. This is not a criticism of my choice, just a light revisiting of how my denial of pain led me into a world that has no happy ending. I watched him break, my hero, losing it. I was petrified. I had to fix him and make sure I put him back together again. A little like Humpty Dumpty, right? All the king's horses and all the king's men couldn't put Humpty Dumpty together again. In reality, there was nothing wrong with my father's brokenness, in fact, this was his time to open his own heart and let pain and devastation in. He did and then, of course, he didn't. To be broken in this world, on our knees with grief, isn't an admirable quality. Men are led to believe they have to hold it together and be tough. It is now fashionable for women to repress their feelings and stay strong, determined, all at the high price of living a real and authentic life. I learned decades later that it takes real bravery to feel all of your feelings and not turn them into emotions. I learned that only the bold-hearted can allow their feelings to pierce them and offer them heaven. All else is an illusion, a seeming attempt at living.

AUTHOR'S NOTE

Even though, and now we all know why, I had no power to change my father, my mother, or anyone else for that matter, I was giving my power away to an unworthy and unholy cause. I was destined to fail. As a failure, a loser in my own mind, I had to venture out into the world and live. What a disaster. My inner world was a mess as I tried to make life work by false principles and I became more and more lost. Anorexia and bulimia were the results. No matter what I did nothing worked, that was the story of my life. It never occurred to me that life was unfolding perfectly and I had turned my back on reality to survive. It wasn't bad, just a sad misunderstanding that caused decades of suffering. As I look back upon my life, my heart opens to the young child and teenager who lost everything that mattered to her in her outside world. At age thirteen, my world changed dramatically, my family was broken apart, my brother and sisters walked out, I was left with two grieving, angry parents and a heart filled with pain and ultimately fear. I did my best, but I did it all wrong.

My father did over the years become the man I always hoped for, he did not deny me this joy as I watched him open and soften in the midst of some of the most painful and unthinkable circumstances. However, this was decades later when he began his own search within. He was a hard man and yet he had an enquiring mind, he found that tiny bit of willingness within that ultimately led him to his humility. He didn't change entirely, yet for me, my father tried, investigated, didn't conform, he was a free thinker. I admired him for this, he instilled the same in many of his children who found their entrepreneurial nature and boldness. Despite his inexcusable behaviour for the most part of his life, his willingness did not go unnoticed. Of course, my mother had a hand in all of this with her enormous heart and determination to soldier on, even in the most challenging of circumstances she never turned to run.

I entered a very challenging life, there was no doubt, for decades I fooled myself and found myself coming up empty; however what we know within will always call us somehow. I found my way back to my own heart. I had a deep longing for Love within, I knew too much to turn my back on what was real for an entire lifetime.

I had many miracles occur in my life, time and time again my life was a testament to what is real and true. I have shared with you some of this in The Power Shift. However the most powerful of all miracles was my connection to my inner gentle, quiet voice. I had access to such a deep and magical goodness and purity it left me breathless at times. This exquisite voice led me to people and reading material that changed my inner world, offering me a path back to my real home, where my only responsibility was to Love and to extend this Love. Love has no opposite, you have no opposite, and it was this realisation that became my beacon. I didn't need to change anyone.

In my mid-thirties I was given a cassette tape by a friend, whose words were: 'I think you are going to like him.' Little was I to know that he was the man that would change my life, offer me the nectar of my own being and see my deeper potential change my life, offer me the nectar of my own being

AUTHOR'S NOTE

and see my deeper potential like no other in this world. I was about to meet another miracle. As I jumped in the car, having picked up the kids, and they jumped in the back, I put the cassette tape into the stereo. We were all buckled in and I was reversing, it was always so busy after school with children and parents everywhere so I took special care. I had fully reversed when I heard his voice coming through the speakers, gentle and soft, it almost sounded like the voice I would hear within. I was flawed, my first thought was, How could such kindness and goodness exist here on this planet? I began to weep, sob without inhibitions. I wasn't sad, I was amazed. I turned and smiled at the little people in the back seat and told them Mummy was fine, just crying. I listened to this tape hundreds of times after this day and every time it took me deeper. I began to realise there was so much to me and therefore others, I began to see clearly. Still to this day I am deeply in love with the stream of Love I found in this tape. Later, there were many more, more words, more understandings, but most importantly of all, more recognition of what matters most.

Is it my deep willingness to know the truth that has brought such incredible people into my life? I have had the honour and the privilege of being supported and deeply helped by wise, awakened beings.

Human beings whose entire lives have demonstrated the Love and goodness we are all seeking in one way or another.

> The Power Shift is my giving back, it is for each of them that I share with you what was once given to me.

HIGHER LOVE

Think about it, there must be higher love
Down in the heart or hidden in the stars above
Without it, life is a wasted time
Look inside your heart, I'll look inside mine
Things look so bad everywhere
In this whole world, what is fair?
We walk blind and we try to see
Falling behind in what could be

Bring me a higher love
Bring me a higher love
Bring me a higher love
Where's that higher love I keep thinking of?

Worlds are turning and we're just hanging on
Facing our fear and standing out there alone
A yearning, and it's real to me

There must be someone who's feeling for me

Things look so bad everywhere
In this whole world, what is fair?
We walk blind and we try to see
Falling behind in what could be

Bring me a higher love
Bring me a higher love
Bring me a higher love
Where's that higher love I keep thinking of?

I will wait for it
I'm not too late for it
Until then, I'll sing my song
To cheer the night along

Bring it...Oh, bring it...

I could light the night up with my soul on fire
I could make the sun shine from pure desire
Let me feel that love come over me
Let me feel how strong it could be

Bring me a higher love
Bring me a higher love
Bring me a higher love
Where's that higher love I keep thinking of?

Written by Steve Winwood and Will Jennings

WHAT IT MEANS

"You choose and the entire universe alters."

Your inner life is where all real change happens. We are moving energy, even when asleep. We move energy through belief and by giving what we are as power to what we believe. Yet imagine for just one moment that you had not a single belief, not even the belief that you are a body with a name. What would you move toward?

Perhaps for a moment, you would simply be Love – peaceful, open and happy, your identity completely undone – just from one tiny glimpse of what is yet to happen.

The Power Shift

You may find this book changes a part of your life or all of it. It may be your introduction to deeper levels of realisation. You may become open to new and unforetold adventures. Either way, it will have served its purpose.

Within the pages of this book, it is my purpose to uncover the inner workings of you, as we paint a tapestry of the very reality we find ourselves in, that it may serve as a guidepost for your life. When you are lost, it's my hope that you will allow these principles to find you; that when you are in need, you will allow reality itself to be your beacon.

Waking up begins with a new perspective, stepping into a new way as you allow the old to fall away, just as a caterpillar transpires from a chrysalis to find her wings in the newness of her existence. This metamorphosis is not a real death – it is a new birth – as she breaks free from a self-created shell. It is a Power Shift. Surrendering in a cocoon of her own making transforms her life. Once she crawled, now she flies. Her power is not used to resist change, but rather she offers her power to the change and in her weakest moment she becomes her true identity, of bright, spectacular colours and delicate beauty. We want to touch the beauty, for her to land on us so we can meet the profound miracle. The caterpillar's willingness allows her to transcend her short, spiky legs and teeny body, to fly. Even for one precious day, she becomes a creature to behold. Of course, the caterpillar could have fought hard against the cocooned walls with her little body against the hard interior 'til death, perhaps bruised and broken without ever knowing her true identity and beauty. Yet I don't believe one has ever fought against its own metamorphosis. So why do we?

What it means

Until you realise, acknowledge, accept and move through, you will continue to feel the outcomes of your life and the powerlessness. You may believe others are the cause of your experiences. You might believe you have no choice when in fact the opposite is true. You move power always, whether you are aware or not. What you give your power to is what matters most. As you come to this realisation, you will finally, and only then, make conscious choices.

The Power Shift initially is moving power – it also acknowledges that happiness does not come from others, but of your inner landscape, your inner choice. Moving is inevitable, you cannot not be moving power.

Reality shows us the way. We don't need to read profound texts or study for decades to know truth. We see it in the smallest and most miraculous of places. Throughout these pages, we will unravel the greatest misunderstandings. This is not the first time this information has been shared. Each teacher has a different flavour and reaches different people. Some hear a message over and over before they can even begin to digest change. Others are afraid, preventing them from considering a power shift. Regardless, this is possible and accessible to everyone. No one is excluded. It doesn't matter how poor, how wealthy, how physically impoverished, educated or illiterate you are, nothing outside of you can prevent you from power shifting. There is no prison cell, relationship or external circumstance that can stop you from making this shift.

The Power Shift

It is possible what you have been desiring all of your life is within these pages. My hope is that you revel in the true principles the universe shares with us.

The Power Shift isn't obscure to most of us.

When you read that you can move your awareness from a negative thought to a positive thought, this is a shift in your power – shifting your power from one point in reality to another.

The five principles here reinforce that you can choose. You choose, you move power; let me repeat this, YOU MOVE POWER! Now we will begin to explore together what this really means and delicately leave behind the notion of positive and negative. We go deeper and find true freedom in the midst of both.

Love, Elle x

A NOTE ON TERMS

Clarity can only occur through a union of meaning between us. When you read a written word, for you to fully understand it, it needs to mean the same to you as it did to me when I wrote this book. For that reason, here is a dictionary of terms.

Reality
Reality is what is, regardless of our opinions. With the absence of all internal resistance, what is left is real. Reality is what is occurring now, as opposed to what we want or believe should be happening now.

Principle
The Power Shift replaces a false principle with a true principle and thereby allows us to see more clearly. Imagine basing

our entire life on a false or fundamentally false source or belief that governs our behaviour. Principles are powerful. As we begin to unlearn the false and adopt true principles, we open new doors. We learn the how.

True Principle

True principles are founded not on fear or self-delusions but on universal law, thereby aligning a human being with reality and empowering them to achieve true happiness and a fulfilled life; an inner life not governed by external circumstances. Every human being has the capacity when living from true principles to live an authentic life.

Power

At its most subtle level, power is your ability to give energy to belief. You direct your energy by first directing your awareness and then by the way in which you relate to what you are aware of.

This is your first power, that of offering energy to belief. In the mastery of this mechanism lies your freedom and liberation. In this mechanism lies a power shift. It is at the heart of how you determine the meaning you see in your world. You are the power keeper, you govern where your power is distributed. How you move will determine the quality of power you will be moving and how aligned or misaligned with reality you are.

You, or I

We have a very particular use of the word 'you' in this book. When referring to 'you' or 'I', what's being referred to is that point in you, within your awareness, that is the tiny master controller of power; the keeper of power, the distributor of power. It's that part of you that is able to subtly feed energy into one thought over another, or into one feeling over another, to one set of meanings or perceptions over another. If you are able to see this point within, let that be your call to a deeper honesty in the way in which you manifest, engage and direct power within. With a greater seeing comes greater responsibility.

Love

When the capitalised version of the word 'Love' is used, it is referring to your true identity, your deeper nature, where you remain unhindered by false beliefs. Love has no identification with experience other than to move in it as tender kindness, clear and free. Love is an unconditional openness and goodness, without effort and for no gain. Love leaves sprinkles of purity everywhere. Some call these miracles.

Love is all that truly exists. When we realise only Love is real, we begin to unfold the greatest mystery we are to ever behold, enriching our life with a deep purpose and meaning, regardless of the circumstances we find ourselves in. Love is perfect. This is the reason you do not need to fix yourself or develop your self-esteem or self-worth. Love is your true nature. You hold the power to be your true nature and also to be otherwise.

Your Secret Rule Book

Reality has its own rule book, based on universal law. True principles exist in alignment with that rule book. At times this may not feel like you wish it to feel or be; however the laws are not negotiable. Nevertheless, you are free to have your own inner rule book containing anything you wish. This secret inner rule book is made up of a myriad of lines that must not be crossed from both yourself and others. We come in with our ancestral, inherited rule book and we add our own pages as we enter our life. The more committed we are to our own rule book, the more easily we will feel offended by others and take situations personally.

At some point you decided to write this rule book and turn away from the universal principles we will learn here.

The Bad, The Guilty, The Shameful
The Seed of All Falsehood and Misunderstanding

The false belief that we are bad, guilty, shameful is buried deep within our subconscious. All of this is found in your glorious little package. The package you entered this world with, ancestral and inherited beliefs, all of them tied up and presented to you. What to do with all of this baggage? That is the question. If you protest and think you don't see yourself in this way, I would challenge you to take a chance and lightly open to the idea for the exercise of this exploration. When we believe in this false belief our power is given to it without question and a lot of power.

Negative Energies

Emotional fear and negativity are all based on false principles, it is a low and dull vibration of energy. It can also be called the shallow mind, superficial and lacking real meaning. Each time you choose what is false you turn your back on reality and its laws, finding yourself in the clutches of weakness and powerlessness. It is where you feel stuck in the past.

Separation

When you perceive your thoughts as real and when you align yourself with these thoughts, you too believe yourself to be separate from your deeper nature. You believe yourself to be a physical body. Your false beliefs in relationships leave you to experience a deep separation, often buried deep within your subconscious, sending out feelings of restlessness, anxiety, fear. Your only way to connect with others and yourself is through experience, experience becomes your reference to your worth and existence. Separation is merely an idea, in reality, you can never be separate from your deeper nature. Love is your source and you can never be separate from what you truly are.

Subtle Bodies

I am not a physicist, nor am I an awakened being. I have awakened countless times to the miracle of what we are and have experienced what we are prior to entering our bodies and of course, what we are without influence from our dense bodies. All levels important to understand, yet our first love must become what is the deepest. The deepest is the closest to your pure source - Love. This body of Love is a subtle body; a level of you. Subtle bodies need stillness and honesty to access. They hold the secrets of the universe and offer untold beauty.

All lack of well-being, mental health issues, unhappiness, broken relationships arise when we anchor ourselves here. You can change your living from coping and surviving and temporary happiness dependent on external experience and conditions, to more real living.

A NOTE ON TERMS

Quantum physicists spend lifetimes proving the existence of what is unseen by our physical eyes and the connectedness of all things, proving the existence of particles and wave forms which never break down, particles of reality and beyond which they agree upon to be the fabric of reality, the fabric of you.

As we follow the Universal Law we find more and more of what is true and step away from our suffering.

PRINCIPLE ONE

False Principle
We deserve perfect love from others.

True Principle
We are Perfect Love; our one joy is in the giving of this Love to others.

A moment long ago, you decided to believe in a false idea and this choice became a part of your inner life – you solidified this belief by repeating it over and over – making you vulnerable to lower and negative energies. All of this occurred when you decided to take on the universe, manipulate its law to fit your personal needs and above all, avoid experiencing what appeared to you as a broken heart. In efforts to protect your heart, you shut down, but in fact, your heart is the doorway to heaven on this Earth. I urge you to reconsider; feelings are fleeting, some feel good and others pierce our hearts, opening us to our true inner life. As we follow the universal law we find more and more of what is true and step away from our suffering. I spent decades building a relationship with my emotions and using them to guide me and by doing this, I destroyed many beautiful relationships and closed off to my inner life. Decades later, I began to realise life and relationships are not meant to make me happy, I must learn how to choose happiness in the midst of the storm of life. The alternative was to live a false life and behold the negativity and fear that become my constant companions.

When you are vibrating at a low and dull vibration you will feel dull and lifeless energies, you will be attracted to the principles they teach and you will demonstrate them to yourself and the world, perpetuating the cycle of what is false. These vibrational energies will tap into your greatest fears, tempting you as they call you to offer them your power, choose me, choose me.

It is time to practise becoming aware of what is going on within. Your emotions may be raging and yet in the midst of the storm, what is most helpful is to ask, 'What do I want right now?' This question is essential because it means that you will be choosing again and not being mastered by old beliefs that no longer serve you and make you suffer. Your

PRINCIPLE ONE

answer may be to apologise, hug a partner, stop being angry with a teenager, or to simply listen for a moment. Soon you will begin to realise nothing in this moment is being threatened. Your peace is always a choice. You shift your power through the intervention of one new thought over another. Feeling trapped in confusion and overwhelm is simply you investing in what is false, handing over your belief and your life to negative energies and reinforcing the belief that you are powerless. We know this is not true. We must learn how to use our power for goodness and happiness and in this, we are walking the path back to our real home within. Even if we remember once a day, once a week, we have begun the shift.

You will never hand over your power to fear and negativity without a hope to fulfil a goal you have already set in your mind. Any goal you have set in the past in a crazy moment will continue to want to be fulfilled whether it brings you happiness or suffering. This is such a sad thought, isn't it? Imagine a heated or unbearable moment when you or someone in your ancestral lineage constructed a belief that was so deeply false and untrue that your life is bound to it. Together we will create the reversal. That is what living in the past means. So it's simple. Every time you are suffering from pain, anger, frustration, overwhelm, to name a few ask yourself, 'What is the goal, the purpose I am trying to achieve now?'

As your belief and power is given to what is true and you step aside from the painful past, you will find it becomes more familiar. Over time, the suffering and restlessness will fade and you will become more comfortable with your true identity.

Relax, this is the part of the journey that is exhilarating because as you begin to move through these pages you will begin to use the principles of truth replacing the immature you.

PRINCIPLE ONE

The choice to align yourself with these false beliefs is hidden deep within your subconscious mind. False beliefs arise from a fear or feelings like shame, humiliation, guilt, heartbreak. Shame and guilt become your foundation among other subconscious beliefs. You see when we begin tuning into the frequency of our ego, a thought stream founded on all that is false, we become enmeshed, confused because we are living our lives based on what is untrue and separate from the universal laws that bring with them a deeply meaningful existence here on Earth. The ego thought system has no reality. What you will learn here will offer you all the tools, principles and strength to undo your investment in the ego and live an authentic life.

Let's go a little further and discover how this all begins. When you have lost your way, you must begin looking for somewhere to anchor – in your search, you find what is most dense as you have lost your connection to your own heart, where your true stability and strength are found. When you are quietly resting in your own heart you are able to feel any amount of pain. We as a species are not limited to the amount of pain or hurt that we have the capacity to feel, otherwise we would have been born defective, not having the capacity to be here. The moment we give our power to the belief that we are unable to feel all of our feelings, fully and completely, that to do so would kill us or maim us somehow, our entire destiny is shifted. We give our power to the belief that we are weak, unable and fearful of our own feelings. In this we turn away from the truth and our own incredible power to feel everything. Our unlimitedness as beings becomes minimized by a false idea. We begin living from within this shell of dishonesty. As you have lost touch with your true identity, you move and feel energy here; after all, feelings and emotions are the energy you seek to navigate through life via experience, leaving you no choice but to seek pleasure and avoid pain. Your power is given to whichever voice promises to protect you from experiencing what you absolutely never want to experience. The energies that speak this language, the language of separation and fear, become familiar and we can become lost, frail, hardened. All lack of well-being, mental health issues, unhappiness, broken relationships arise when we anchor ourselves here. You can change your living from coping and surviving and temporary happiness dependent on external experience and conditions, to more real living. A new willingness through the use of your true principles to be more, and most importantly, begin to Love more. False beliefs are aligned with the false idea of winning; life is a fight, a competition and you are always in the game. Isn't this idea itself exhausting? What could there possibly be outside of us that we are willing to give over our happiness and peace for?

Reality has its own rule book based on true principles offering us the opportunity to experience different levels of its infinite nature. You have such a plethora of choice to give your power to. At different times in your life, you may see the suffering your choices are causing and wisely change your course.

When you come into the world as a baby, so does both your conscious and subconscious mind. You do not enter just as a body. There are many layers of you and your mind is al-

We may view our brokenness as weakness – this ideology could not be further from the truth.

ready harbouring so much. Within your mind you are aware and you are unaware of the beliefs. As you grow, you become aware of the subconscious being like a storage space on your hard drive; it holds everything, the good, the bad and the infinite.

Over time you define yourself by your beliefs and the more identified you are by your beliefs the stronger you will hold them. This makes for a very opinionated person, after all, your opinions become who you believe you are. We don't always remember consciously what we believed as toddlers, teenagers, young adults, otherwise, we would be hardened and inflexible and we wouldn't grow. Nonetheless, it is these conflicting beliefs that cause our suffering until we realise we have the power to release what no longer serves us and mature.

As a child, our mind over time, becomes fractured by our wants and needs. Human beings, no matter their size or their age, have the potential to move their power, either offering it to what they know is true or what they need or want. One is honest, the other self-centered. When a child is a baby, it's use of power is law. It cries it is fed, changed, pampered, all its wants and needs met, in most cases. As the baby begins to grow up, it continues to give its power to one way of being or the other. Over time it decides moment by moment to offer its power to what in the moment seems best. It cannot stop this as much as it can stop trying to walk. Just because the giving of our power to one belief or another cannot be seen it doesn't mean it isn't happening. It has to exercise the use of power to learn how to use it. And who is going to help teach a baby how

PRINCIPLE ONE

to use its power in a healthy and meaningful way? Uh-oh! In a child's mind, the parent is their God. Since birth, these people have kept it alive, loved it and now the real work begins.

As parents, we are not perfect and we too are learning how to love in a mature way. So it is obvious that our children will be a little messy. Relax, this is the part of the journey that is exhilarating because as you move through these pages you will begin to use the principles of truth to kindly replace the immature parts of yourself with new found wisdom and honesty. Your children and loved ones will benefit. You cannot know what you don't know so let's put the guilt aside and demonstrate mature love to ourselves and to those around us.

A child, just like you once were, through experience and choice will feel hurt, in a human body this is unavoidable. What it does with this hurt in its own mind will matter. Let me share my life so you can see how it works.

I was born into a family of six children, my mother was downtrodden, poor and suffering from depression. My experience of my early life was of being neglected and unloved, the hurt so devastating it even affected me physically. I was a very sickly child. Sickness, in fact, was when I had my mother all to myself. Wow, this is amazing to share, feeling the vulnerability is so healing and kind. The years went by and my mother became consumed by her burdens. I found my needs unmet. I felt neglected more and more and I turned away from her and therefore my own heart. The hurt and pain was too much, my attempts at getting what I thought

If we open ourselves to the use of a true principle in a difficult moment we blossom in our inner world, finding pockets of joy and happiness, natural to an inner state which does not shut down. We change immediately in this moment.

PRINCIPLE ONE

I needed from her failing repeatedly, and I was in despair. I tried everything, I threw tantrums, I became a fussy eater, all to no avail. I came to the conclusion that I was bad and therefore unlovable. My new beliefs were used to hide the underlying beliefs that I was a failure and of no value in my subconscious and now I had a new identity. I was bad but at least I felt powerful and I could work with this. It made me moody, unhappy and needy, but at least it felt better. It felt as though I had control and solved my painful experience of feeling powerless. Of course the cost I paid for this false sense of power was extremely high.

My heart was closed and I had hard thoughts, negativity and fear became real to me. I turned into my own mother, even though I had turned away from her. I had turned away from my own inner beauty, my own heart, by believing I couldn't or wouldn't be with this hurt and pain, I was effectively saying that reality and the experiences it was presenting me were wrong. When we turn our backs on our ability to feel hurt and pain, we turn our backs on our own hearts.

It took me decades to undo this identity, it ate into my life and left me bereft until I knew life wasn't the problem.

As you continue to choose your beliefs, whatever they are, you will look for reinforcement of them in the world and in others. What use is a belief if you cannot prove it to be true? Your mind will have it as a goal to keep repeating and achieving.

Now here is the good part. You see, the child, the immature part of you, believes that one day it will master this hurt and pain. To do so it continues to attract situations allowing it to re-experience the same belief that one day it will conquer, be loved and finally it will win. This is the false belief that keeps us trapped in meaningless and painful lives. All we need to do is stop and ask, 'What do I really want now?' It has to begin with one false belief that in turn opens up the labyrinth of all false beliefs founded on fear and lack. When you take the thread extended to you when you are in the labyrinth, you begin to find your way out of the false and into what is true. Just like Ariadne offers Theseus the thread to escape the labyrinth after defeating the Minotaur, you too can take the thread I extend to you now and begin unravelling.

When in the midst of anger you open your heart, you will feel like crying. This is because anger is a form of control you use to protect your own vulnerability. Without it shielding you, you will be open to feeling everything you were using to cover it up. In this, your heart will take you to a place within your inner world that you have been missing, you will begin to find your true inner life. The idea that crying or being heartbroken must be avoided is false. We may view our brokenness as weakness – this ideology could not be further from the truth. Our world is a testament to this, look around you, furthermore look at the statistics for pharmaceutical drug use for unhappy people, it is on the rise. This idea, this false idea doesn't work.

Perhaps in a moment of madness, you forgot you were a constant beaming light on the movie screen and replaced your true identity with a false one. You began to feel the self-importance of being an individual character with power

PRINCIPLE ONE

and personal will, so you shifted your belief onto this false identity and began to construct an identity based on you being the lead role in life. Yet, nothing changed, the light didn't change. You became a person in a body separate from all other bodies, in a life you either loved or hated. You constructed opinions which developed over time from your feelings and your experiences and you lost contact with your inner light, your true identity. Your vibration changed as you believed what was false and your vibration became lower and dull, and this frequency attracted the same in others searching for the same as you. Now, alongside others with a similar belief in lack, you begin to try over and over to get what you think you do not have externally. The light within continues to vibrate at a frequency of great beauty and yet you no longer believed in the light, it was hidden from your view by your own shrouded beliefs.

In this moment of madness, you went against the universal laws and decided to take charge of the universe. It's a big call. You built a new reality based on what was false and are probably now still giving it your best shot. Yet life and reality are not yours to control, this effort and trying is often leaving you feeling despondent, powerless and very controlling of others, passively or outwardly. The need to control your external world comes from believing your happiness and purpose exists outside of you.

The want to be loved is the driving force behind the construction of the false beliefs, wanting to be something other than infinite Love. When did infinite Love become not enough? The problem is we believe we have a way, but sadly

Your highest purpose is to reverse what is false through withdrawing your power from it and give all of your power to the true principles that are aligned with universal laws.

PRINCIPLE ONE

this way founded on false principles leads us down a path where true fulfilment and Love can never be found. You become vulnerable to negativity because you are already standing on false ground. You feel trapped, powerless, helpless, as you embrace this ideology and begin to vibrate at a frequency aligned with what you believe. The longing within to be loved and accepted and to be worthy all handed over to what is outside of you, making you hand your power to these false principles. The false wants to take charge of reality when this is an impossible task.

When you are believing this, you have at one moment in time chosen to turn away from reality and its true principles. You have chosen to turn away from the universal laws. You may ask, 'Why, why would I do such a thing?' I compel you to not wonder what happened but look towards what you can now do to unlearn and undo what was once falsely constructed in your mind. You don't need to understand why, if why is important you will find this answer. The conditioned and patterned frequencies within that keep you limited and separated from your deepest essence, from LOVE, can be reversed, unlearned and you can begin to see once they had an assigned purpose, now they have none.

If we open ourselves to the use of a true principle in a difficult moment we blossom in our inner world, finding pockets of joy and happiness, natural to an inner state which does not shut down. We change immediately in this moment.

By power shifting, we feel a new level of clarity, energy, strength. Shutting down our hurt shuts down our inner world and brings with it an alliance to fear and lack, leaving our minds attuned to lower vibrations and energies. We become anxious and restless.

Your self-created rulebook is founded on beliefs, some inherited and many you have picked up along the way, perpetuated by a desire to be the ruler of your kingdom, the author of your life. When you live by your secret rule book you will have a self-importance fuelled by childlike needs and wants. Even if such needs and wants are false, you will be bound to false principles because they build the stories that feed your rule book.

Everyone we meet in this world has their own rule book, they too have written and inherited beliefs. As the rule books clash so do relationships and hopes and dreams are destroyed. Reality is so much kinder. Even in the most devastating of life circumstances, there is a kindness that pervades in moving with reality.

Unlike the caterpillar that crawls, unaware she will soon emerge from her chrysalis into a butterfly with new powers and abilities, we human beings do know what our true purpose is – yet it takes us very little time to forget. We become enmeshed in feelings, emotions and thoughts and our true purpose becomes repressed. We believe we are the creator of our own individual purpose. This couldn't be further from the truth, it is a false belief. For our lives to hold the highest meaning, the highest purpose must always come first. We are not the creator of our highest purpose. When we turn away from our true purpose we suffer the consequences.

The caterpillar cannot forget or develop a new plan for her species. The human being definitely can and when guided by false beliefs does exactly that. Suddenly, your life is about how you feel and how you don't want to feel, it becomes about what you can have and what you think you cannot have. You become consumed by your needs and your true purpose is dormant as if it never existed.

When we turn away from our true purpose we leave behind our golden palace in search of crumbs. You see, at one time in your life your wants and needs became more important than your true purpose – you decided to close your heart and in that moment you chose a false belief. You identified with lack, not having enough, and from this false belief, you built a life. The false principles became your allies.

When you are anxious and suffering the emptiness in your heart keeps calling and your mind is always reeling. Your life first must be accepted as it is, embraced, all of it, even the parts that hurt and cause you pain. It is only from this space you can open to change. Every time you wish it was different you lock it in. Our first true principle holds the key to finding our way out of the maze. Our golden thread is always hanging nearby, all we need to do is to reach out and take it, we are never alone or deserted. We have everything we need to find our way back home.

You have nothing to fear, hurt and pain are the doorway to your heart.

As you reverse your use of power from the five false principles to five true principles you will say goodbye to the old and you will begin to access your lifelong wishes – true happiness and peace. Happiness and peace are not dependent on others or life circumstances. Your roots will grow deep into the Earth and you will find your branches begin to expand and your tree will blossom, sharing its beauty with the world.

You will use your power towards a true principle, find a new love for yourself with dignity and self-respect. Self-worth and value doesn't come from others, it is the fruit of deep roots and flowering through the honest use of your power. Husbands, boyfriends, friends, children will all be grateful to know you and this world will be fortunate to have you. You can create an abundance of purpose in your life and take specific actions to achieve them, this is the exquisite nature of being a human being. Nevertheless, if your highest purpose doesn't come first you will be micro-managing your life in the hope of fulfilling these purposes, making them mean more than they actually do. When we are identified with our goals and visions we block our available clarity and cause ourselves meaningless stress.

Your highest purpose is to reverse what is false through withdrawing your power from it and give all of your power to the true principles that are aligned with universal laws. I don't know about you but taking on the universe is a big call, one I have exhausted myself trying to do for decades. I would rather work with it, wouldn't you?

If your highest purpose is to reverse what is false, one thing is for sure, looking outside of yourself is completely false. You see, why your first purpose must come first for you to live honestly is because you hold all of the power.

Apologising became a sign of strength and commitment to truth for me, I began to see the humility and how it quietly and kindly connected me with my heart and gently showed my commitment to change.

The Power Shift is calling!

Life is an exquisite opportunity and we learn as we go. We choose, again and again. This realisation is the beginning of what is now a fresh perspective.

I don't want to get philosophical here, but you see there is also within you a goodness, the stream in us that knows what works, what is good and yet because we don't have the true principles to use throughout our life, we give our power over to thought streams that truly do not serve us. It is as if we have access to a wellspring of energies; false, good, lower, higher, real. As the power-keeper of our experience, learning that we have this inherent power is learning who we really are and that we are the holders of power.

We are not powerless.
Only when you adopt this knowledge will you begin to realise the miraculous nature of you.
You have the power to move energy.
You are the power-keeper.
You choose how to move your power.

In your push for superficial wants and needs, your purpose you will go to the highest bidder. You will see yourself as a limited physical self and condemn others to achieve your own needs. This is how you move when you are living dishonestly and have adopted false principles about you. Hon-

PRINCIPLE ONE

esty wakes you up to a different purpose here, a forgotten purpose, yet so intrinsically woven into the tapestry of your experience. You will then have the opportunity to accept it or not. This is how powerful you are. This deeper purpose rests on your belief, on your waking up from the slumber of your existence. As you begin to see you have hoodwinked yourself into believing what is false as a young child and thus offered your infinite power to false principles, you will begin to steer the ship to paradise, leaving behind false notions of fear and a small, limited idea of what you are and how you are able to be in your life.

All of the energies seem to exist here, we are learning which ones are true and which ones to overlook, for the sake of truth.

As we step back into our principles here, both false and true, we will explore what control means. The principle of control can be very positive when we are not misusing it. The only true form of control that exists lies in your withdrawal of power from what is false.

Let me share something with you and show you once again how truth offers you all the miracles you have been looking for outside of yourself.

My relationship with my first husband was destined to fail, not from a lack of love or goodness but simply because of a lack of true principles in our daily life. We were young and had no idea how to choose between what was false and what was true, needless to say, we were living out the Disney model of love. Could I have changed the destiny of my bond with my husband? Yes, I can see this now. Nonetheless, our choices left us moving apart. This is not a guilt, shame, blame situation, it's just wisdom and insight looking back with kindness and accepting the facts. We are used to describing why something didn't work by going into the behaviours of others and ourself, our needs and wants not being met by the other. Why do we do this when there is a much simpler answer? Our habitual way of trying to figure out what went wrong is to look at the behaviour of others and ourself and yet in this misunderstanding, we are missing what really offers us the opportunity to build a beautiful relationship and life. The reversal of the false and the embracing of the true. The simplicity of this answer will never do when your purpose is to continue to remain in the cycle of hurt. I know it sounds crazy. The choice we once made to adopt false principles is crazy when we have access to infinite joy within; however, life cannot lie. As we look outside of us we see what we have chosen and value – it is this very misunderstanding that needs to change. Remember, recreating childhood hurts can't be avoided. Life keeps offering us the same, over and over until we turn the false into the true. Herein we change our destiny.

My choices even as a child left me suffering. Needless to say, it worked heavily against me for decades and damaged many relationships and endeavours, most importantly my own connection to what I loved more than all else, truth. I remember telling my father as a six-year-old that what we were experiencing at home wasn't real love. He would look at me quizzically, trying to figure me out, he did this for years until later in his life he confessed his thoughts and out of the blue said, 'You are special, Elle, not everyone knows the things you know about love.' To have heard these words at another time of my life would have inflated me, yet that day I had no need for my father's acceptance and approval for I had found my own validation within, and maybe that's why he shared when he did. Our life has a way of offering us confirmation when we embrace it first, it reflects and offers us our wishes when we least need to hear them. What a beautiful paradox. Back to the story, you see even though as a little girl I knew there was another way, I had a deep inkling of real Love and I had forgotten what real Love meant. I had even hijacked a truth about Love and turned it into a false principle. I had completely turned my back on what real Love was and completely focused on my outermost world for my happiness. Trying with all of my will to get it from my external world, my mental health diminished, peace and happiness eluded me and in this misuse of power, I became lost. I was in tatters. Others saw a different version of me and yet within my own experience, I was a total failure and still waiting for my life to be better. Can you see the misunderstanding here? As I write this, my whole heart opens and I love that I get to see into what was, without an ounce of judgement, guilt or shame.

Your life doesn't need to change, you need to make a power shift, that's it.

Relationships were always a significant part of my life, perhaps more so than for most people. Even as a child I took them seriously. I always had an innate ability to tune into others and sadly I had focused my safety and my happiness on what was occurring outside. I adopted this misunderstanding, making the false principle of controlling others real. I used it incessantly and therefore misused my power to fulfil the belief that my happiness and safety was in the hands of others. It never worked and my own choice to misuse my power in this way led me to recreate childhood hurts over and over until the pain became too great and I had to look for another way. Luckily for me, the way was true and my relationships with others and myself became deeply intimate and real. My favourite word was 'sorry'. I decided to say sorry each time I noticed I had made a mistake. Apologising became a sign of strength and commitment to truth for me, I began to see the humility and how it quietly and kindly connected me with my heart and gently showed my commitment to change. In recent times, I began to use this method again, when I noticed I had stepped away from my own heart. We cannot always avoid misusing our power but we can acknowledge it and put an end to it by choosing again. The power of the word 'sorry' is profound, it is a little like forgiveness; when shared honestly it simply allows you to step into a kindness rather than blame. Remember, as we misuse our power we enter the realm of the false and the lower streams in this universe and open the door to all negative emotions and thought streams. Therefore sorry said with love and honesty is a simple acknowledgement of you seeing what you have once again done and just simply stopping. Do it once and your life will change, do it twice and

PRINCIPLE ONE

you will open new doors within that you never knew you had access to. Love is waiting for you to reclaim it!

As you stay connected with your own inner world, your true inner guide will quietly confirm the truth of the next few sentences. It may feel like a tiny murmur, this is how you begin to reconnect with your true inner guide by listening in stillness and quiet.

This energy that moves power isn't outside of you working against you or for you, it is in fact 'you', you are moving power through belief. When you are truly honest nothing is clearer. Our attachment to the belief that there are forces outside of us with power to create our life is yet another misunderstanding. Consider this for a moment, you are not afraid of a lack of power but rather the realisation of your power. If you were to accept this as true, how many beliefs would no longer serve you? How many beliefs would you need to erase from your secret inner rule book? How happy would you become and how free would you feel? It would literally be as though you had a bolt cutter and snapped through the chains that have shackled you for years.

It becomes extremely obvious our belief is where power will move, the universal laws are simple and uncompromising. As we continue with my story, you too may begin to see what you want more than anything else in this world.

Relationships came and went, I had no idea how to choose a partner but I was learning. Relationships became my way back home and it is still the same. Let's skip an entire decade of complete mayhem. In my attempt to find my way back (what a crazy ride!), my tiny little bit of willingness to put the rule book down had to prevail.

At forty-two years of age, I met Toby. Finally, I had worked out how to make my life work. I owned a successful business, had amazing friends, clients, team members. I was happy. Life still had its challenges but I had built an inner stability and had a deep faith and trust in reality and how it played out in my life. I had worked diligently and applied the true principles to my life. I had gained a new level of respect from those in my world and loved seeing how my true use of power was reflected in my outside world. I was independent and strong and the best was yet to come. You see I still didn't have all the pieces of the jigsaw puzzle.

I came to see my life wasn't about working life out. It still isn't.

The next phase of my life was about unlearning all the blocks to Love I had built within my mind and finding a deep intimacy, a bond with another. I wanted it more than anything else in the whole world, I just didn't know how to get it. Even though I had entered a new level of success and happiness in my life, the next chapter of my life was a mystery to me. All of my false principles were about to resurface with a vengeance – not straight away, but over the next ten years.

I had booked flights to an event in Brisbane and I invited a dear friend to join me. My favourite teacher had arrived for

Forgiveness wasn't necessary. What had happened was a miracle, as I moved my power honestly, choosing once again a true principle. In this newness, I had become stronger and had new ground within to deepen any relationship.

The Power Shift

four days and I wasn't going to miss it. I missed my children, I had such a strong bond with them, even if we had our difficulties they were my life. I could always see them deeply. I knew whatever I learnt during this time away would benefit my relationship with them, this event was all about truth and I was so ready for more. Toby and I met there, having arrived from the same city, and we soon became friends. There were no sparks, no chemistry, not even a notion of anything more than a deep dear friendship. He was eleven years younger than me. He was stable, the type that is loyal and committed (not my type at all!). Toby had recently separated and after our return home, we began to share time together. I would cook dinner and he would listen. He didn't own a mobile phone when we met, surprising for a tech-head. I lived in a beautiful heritage building behind my studio with no doorbell. So the only way for Toby to let me know he had arrived was to find a public phone box and call me. I loved it! Of course, it didn't take long for him to buy a mobile phone, but in the meantime, thank goodness for Telstra. Toby, in the beginning, wasn't a big talker but a great listener. During this time I had begun seeing someone else and we talked about my relationship among other things. Toby was so kind and sweet and open, his friendship meant the world to me. We got along. I began to set up dates for Toby with some of my single friends. He was not interested at all. There was never a murmur about us being together until the day I received an email and our entire lives changed. Toby had reached out and shared his feelings, it wasn't a choice. I knew it was inescapable.

PRINCIPLE ONE

No sparks, no chemistry, everything seemed unusually uneventful yet somehow we had the foundations. I loved Toby deeply and for the first time, I felt as though there was nothing I wanted to change, he was perfect. Of course, the need to change him came later. As two extremely strong people with strong rule books, our relationship was not easy and the more we wanted to hang on to our own rule books the tougher it became. This is how relationships can be, an opportunity to see our own blocks to what we really want, to give Love to another no matter what. In the difficult times, I withdrew wounded and unhappy and Toby continued on unwavering. It was as if the ultimate destruction, the burning of our rule books needed to happen first. Over time we began to see what we ultimately wanted, how deep our bond and our love had grown, yet it was the miracles for me that changed my ultimate purpose.

As the years rolled on our life became an extraordinary adventure, each of us realising our inner gifts and abilities. We became less inclined to want to change the other and accept we could love each other even if we were different on the surface. I still struggled. I was being undone, my rule book was turning to ashes and it was in my willingness to allow this we found our deepest connection.

One day years into our relationship we were having a conversation, and I spoke of an issue I had with Toby, as the false me did, focusing again outside of myself. It was a false way of connecting with another and yet it was still not visible to me. During these times I wasn't aware I was misusing my power by false principle, but I was. My need for connection

When we look for answers outside of ourselves, the world will always offer us a temptation for a temporary fix.

and love was still playing itself out in my life, recreating old childhood hurts, again and again, hoping this time I would succeed. Toby wouldn't have it and in his own frustration shared his view of me. BOOM! I was stopped. His words (not that I can even remember them now) hit me so hard that I felt like I would never recover. If he had repeated them to another person they may have said, 'Yeah right, I don't think so, mate.' I felt crushed. Toby went out and I sat on my bed, numb. I knew the only way to move past this was to reach out to one of my mentors, someone I trusted to tell me the truth. I didn't have friends who told me what I wanted to hear, those alliances were well and truly gone. My friends and mentors, I trusted to always open doorways even if it was painful to accept, they were my true friends.
I made the call and James answered.

I shared what happened with him and he listened. I was surprisingly calm, even though I was shattered within, thinking, How would I ever recover? I remember telling him this and then I heard his quiet and kind words, 'Oh, I see what's happened, you are believing the lie of the ego.' Bam, the light went on in my mind and the doorway burst open. He didn't go into psychoanalysis and trying to fix me, just one statement aligned me with what was actually happening. I was giving my power to a false belief. I was clear it was a lie and all that remained was to release it. Toby was no longer present, my salvation was not dependent on him, but on me. I finally knew how to use my power truthfully and I did.

I began to loosen up within, my mind cleared and I began to feel the pain in my heart of a false belief, a lie I had

A pattern is a sequence that repeats.
When we choose to believe something, over time it becomes a groove, a pattern in our energetic system and our nervous system.

held onto for decades, maybe even longer. As it began to release, I experienced the piercing in my heart and it felt uncomfortable and painful as the negative thoughts associated with this belief, the stream of thinking that held it all together began spilling over: Who was to blame? How will I retaliate? What must I do to justify my anger? I stayed with the pain which became sweeter and easier to bear and ignored the negative thoughts. I decided to undo this lie. I knew it no longer served a purpose in my life, I was giving it up. I found myself in the hurt and beneath it was Love. I thanked James. I sat on the balcony allowing the energy, labelled as pain to move through and I opened the door and stepped into a new knowledge, new principles and my rule book couldn't enter. I was given a fresh beginning and realised Toby was my golden ticket to all of my shutdown doorways to heaven. In fact, everyone in my life was. I began to reawaken honesty and listen to the delicate quiet voice I had learnt to love and trust years ago. As I listened, I knew pain and hurt was not about what others say, it was about what we are already believing in our falseness about ourselves, their words touching the lies, and instead of using these tiny touches to open locked doors we project our pain outwardly onto the other.

On this day, my heart opened and opened and opened and Love was pouring through me. I was grateful for Toby and for his words alongside the gift they offered me to see what I was holding onto. My relationship had a deeper purpose, a true purpose finally. I wasn't afraid of hurt or pain. I finally had found the code to its undoing. I didn't need to keep using it to justify my anger or my rightness, but rather to unlearn and undo the blocks I had constructed between myself and the world. Toby returned with a bunch of flowers in his hand and my love for him felt new. He was no longer someone that could at times hurt me, cause me pain, I felt a new level of connection with him, more space and depth. It was a defining moment as I began the new adventure of true intimacy in all my relationships. He apologised for his words, I thanked him for what he had said and told him he had done nothing wrong. Forgiveness wasn't necessary. What had happened was a miracle, as I moved my power honestly, choosing once again a true principle. In this newness, I had become stronger and had new ground within to deepen any relationship. I was immersed in a Love bubble for months on end, this new level of honesty revealed my true nature and as it entered my life everything changed.

We went on to grow, build, deepen and flourish in our relationship. At times we forgot and our rule books reappeared, yet it takes little time to kindly lay them aside and find each other once again. We decided on what came first and what was most important and used our true principles to solve all our challenges.

In this story, once again from a childhood hurt that I had re-experienced over and over, in the past choosing many times the false principle of blame, shame and guilt. The solution was always to separate, be right, dividing me in my mind and experience. There is nothing anyone can do to us, no

PRINCIPLE ONE

matter how deeply painful, that has the power to prevent us from our own true nature. The true principles are the teachers that guide us as we learn how to be with hurt and pain and still continue to blossom and toss aside the need for blame, shame and guilt. The false principles I chose to live by and give my power to taught me over and over to react and shut down my doorways to Love, but the painful words became the least of my problems. What was most painful was the shutting down of my inner world, the choice to ignore Love.

Fear to feel is the first reason for us to ever choose wrongly. The very moment we resist a feeling we are opening up a stream of negativity. This inner thought stream will feed you junk thoughts and you will experience the consequence of such thinking. It is the same as if you ate junk food every day for the rest of your life. What would happen to your physical and mental health? This negative thought stream is founded on false principles and therefore its curriculum for living is all wrong. Would you send your child to a school whose curriculum was founded on false principles of physics, mathematics, science, English? How would you expect your child to pass exams and achieve academically without the true principles? It is impossible and you would never do it. When it comes to true principles for living our lives we fall terribly short and sadly teach our children all that we know that is often so terribly wrong. False principles are founded on blame, shame and guilt, projection and of course your need to control, change, micromanage your world. Your success and happiness is dependent on your achievements, manifestation of your dreams and of course, it will constantly tell you that you need fixing, changing, improving. You have opened the doorway to this stream of thought and will be offered short-term fixes and addictions. One thing it will never do is set you free, you need to want to reverse the falseness more than anything else.

Somehow, along the way, we believed to feel pain or hurt was wrong and we had to avoid these feelings at all costs. On the flip side, we believed those good feelings were to be sought after, making us trapped in this false world. More of what feels good and avoidance of what feels bad. The inner stresses this creates leave us experiencing a restlessness and over time, this can affect our well-being and mental health. We resist and judge our bad feelings, believing the lie that we are powerless and weak against them. We want nothing more than to be rid of them. In fact, nothing is further from the truth. With practice, we realise the bad feelings we have tried to avoid for decades when allowed to move through our own hearts will reveal our real strength and true identity. Indeed, it is the lie that to feel is a weakness that left us experiencing this need to take control and avoid feeling helpless and powerless. The lie we built against our own wellspring of infinite Love, joy, freedom.

When we look for answers outside of ourselves, the world will always offer us a temptation for a temporary fix. Sadly, pharmaceuticals have become attractive not only for adults but for the younger people of our world. You are not helpless, you are able to feel all of your feelings, the good, the bad and the ugly. At first, you might fail over and over again, and even have the thought that you can't do it repeat-

PRINCIPLE ONE

ing itself incessantly. The closer you get to changing a pattern, releasing yourself from fear just a little more each time, is where you will find the voices getting louder and stronger. Power that has been offered to a pattern over time is not easily reversed, it does take a tiny bit of willingness each time to lean in to what you want more than fear and suffering. Lean in to your own longing for Love and ask your inner guide for help. Call out for help when it feels as though you are failing as it is in the failure when you get to choose again.
You are never alone.

Your true inner guide is waiting for you to reclaim your belief.

You choose and your power follows your belief. This is universal law.

There are no fines for not abiding by this law. There are energies and thought streams you will become vulnerable to the moment you veer away from what is true. There are only two choices that you have in this life, false or true, everything else is out of your hands.

Let's look at beliefs and patterns. A pattern is a sequence that repeats. When we choose to believe something, over time it becomes a groove, a pattern in our energetic system and our nervous system. The pattern has momentum and repeats itself over and over, we feel powerless against the momentum and the pattern is like an addiction to food, alcohol, drugs, sex, pain, self-harming ... the list goes on. Our addiction to anything tells us that we have lost control. If we try to change a pattern of behaviour to our addiction we will always lose. The behaviour isn't the cause, the cause is found

Life doesn't lie, it perfectly offers us all we need to undo the false and allow more of what is true to enter our lives.

PRINCIPLE ONE

in the belief that perpetuates the behaviour. Belief, good or bad, true or false, has the power you have given to it, it will attract reinforcement and confirmation. Have you heard the statement: What you believe is what you will become? The law of the universe works one way and belief is key and an essential piece of this life curriculum we are learning.

Believe in your power to choose. You are actually doing it subconsciously anyway, and in every belief, whether a lie or the truth, you have invested your power. It is time to reclaim it.

This book isn't a curriculum about why we turn away from the infinite intelligence or why we must Love what we first are. We are here to begin believing in something other than the false and entering into philosophical questions and answers may distract us. There will be plenty of time to get the answers you might find helpful in the future. For now, even the idea that we choose our inner reactions is big enough. Even if it is true, we have spent such a long time believing and therefore doing the opposite that it may take some unlearning to really see the truth of this principle. To expect perfection here is yet another step in the wrong direction, only kindness and gentleness is helpful now. As you watch a baby learn to walk, it is with the same innocent loving kindness you must enter The Power Shift. You do not need kindness, support, love or care from anyone outside of you, you must offer it to yourself first.

To be brave enough to reflect on principle one is really a huge leap forward, you don't have to agree, but to at least be open to reflect is wonderful. So as we look into this principle my hope is that you stay open and allow yourself to imagine a deeper meaning for your life and a purpose filled with possibility.

If we decide to introduce a true purpose into our lives we begin to see that time offers new value; other human beings no matter how intimate or not have a new meaning in our lives, our moments are no longer there to be filled with mindless thinking but to offer us a path to our evolution. This Earth offers all of its inhabitants an exquisite purpose when adopted first it reveals a deep meaningful experience on this planet regardless of the chaos we are faced with here.

When our purpose is not rooted in false principles, we don't see the world as a place that exists only to serve our needs and wants. We also gain a new way of being, where we find ourselves living without the disappointment of 'no', and instead live with the delight of 'yes'. We are free to live in this reality regardless of what we face.

This knowledge is part of our evolution, remembering what our purpose is holds an entirely different meaning. When we come from our true purpose we don't have a problem with reality as it arises. This is a frightening thought initially because our false principles are founded on us gaining control over our life. Reality is powered naturally by the way the universe moves forward, always forward. It is a little like a duck; a duck never looks back, in fact, it is very difficult for it to turn its head so it is always wobbling forward. It is the same for reality, even though we feel and experience in our mind and our bodies that we are being pushed back, attacked from the outside – this is false. When we believe these false

PRINCIPLE ONE

principles we inadvertently demonstrate them to each other and our children, reinforcing them repeatedly.

You move your power by what you are believing in any given moment, you would by now have read this countless times. You can choose the false principles and open up a cavern of negativity and fear, this is inevitable, or you can choose a true principle and move power honestly. It sounds so easy, right? Well the truth is there is a lot of work here and deep-rooted patterns are never easy to uproot, the good news is you built the entire false reality, so guess what? You can now demolish the whole goddam building! I know right now you don't really believe that you are the power-keeper and that you are choosing; this principle sounds like a great idea and there may even be a part within you that wishes to believe, but right now you believe you have too much to lose, unless you were like me and had nothing to lose. Anxiety, fear, overwhelm, feeling drained, being emotional, depressed and losing control are all examples of how false principles affect our daily lives. You can also take into account your physical body and issues you may be having with health and wellness. True principles always offer you a smoother journey and clarity which can help you when suffering physically. Your infinite intelligence is always available to you; learning how to listen and how to access it is one powerful shift you will make as you begin to reverse the use of your power from the false to what is true.

How do we know when a true principle is in action and we are giving our power to it? The answers are easy, you will experience a new level of calm in the midst of any storm; you will experience a new level of peace as you begin to choose true principles over and over, and you will feel happiness rising up for no apparent reason. You will know a new level of aliveness even when things are not going your way and your mind will be clearer. You will find strength in your choices and as you begin to like being this person you are, you may find the outside world likes you too. Your relationships will enter new levels of depth and openness, love will find a new flow and you will create new patterns in your world.

The gifts to the ones who live aligned with true principles are endless.

PRINCIPLE TWO

False Principle
Other people and circumstances are the cause of my choices and behaviour.

True Principle
I am choosing my own feelings and behaviours

When we give our power to false principles over and over and over again, it creates momentum. The false principle 'Other people and circumstances cause my choices and behaviour' definitely has momentum. Let's see why. When we adopt a belief as truth, we become bound to it. We give it reality, even though it is false. It has been given power by our belief and over time it becomes our identity, our reality. We no longer see ourselves as infinite intelligence and Love. Every belief creates connections, some unseen and some seen, we cannot escape from our beliefs and nor should we be afraid to confront them.

Life doesn't lie, it perfectly offers us all we need to undo the false and allow more of what is true to enter our lives. Through our belief, we move and our power moves. We are not helpless to create change to see a different world. As we embrace a truth that we are responsible for how we use our power, we begin to reprogram our energetic system and our physical nervous system. When we simply forget and fall back into the old false principle we can say sorry, forgive ourselves inwardly and choose anew. This is the express highway to freedom. The true use of your power is an immediate change.

As you begin to embrace this principle you may hear a murmur within calling for your power. Ignore it and thus you will withdraw your belief and redirect your power. This old patterning is like an old broken record, and your investment, as you give over your power to what you know is worthy of it, may cry and scream to have some of it back. Yet it is time now to choose wisely and love that change. After all, it doesn't matter how it feels, what is most important is what you now choose to believe. Throughout this transformation there will be many times you choose to close your heart. What is important is to merely notice with honesty and pass your power back to what you know the value of once again.

If somebody left you when you were hoping for a proposal, your heart breaks and you choose to depress, you are choosing to depress. Remember we can choose to feel hurt without a story, this prevents depression, so the key is to learn how to feel our feelings without needing to shut down or enter a narrative that served in the past to stop us from feeling.

Hurt with a story is depression, hurt on its own is just hurt, it comes and it goes without shutting you down or building false beliefs about hurt. Life is about feeling, we feel all the time, even when we dream. To avoid feelings of any kind is to enter a false world where you believe you can control reality by the use of false principles. Feelings connect us deeply to our inner world.

The Power Shift is your life curriculum.
The Power Shift offers you all you've forgotten.
The Power Shift is the path to reclaim your true use of power.

Negative emotions when unhindered simply vanish in a timely fashion, as you leave them untouched you withdraw your power and reclaim what serves. As you turn your back kindly without resistance or judgement on your old false principles and beliefs you will notice you have access to two worlds, one where guilt, shame and blame are the masters and another where infinite Love and intelligence are present. Which do you choose?

If you begin bringing this idea to your day, say to yourself: I am choosing overwhelm right now. I am choosing anger right now. I am choosing sadness right now. Tell yourself over and over until you begin to see where you are placing your power, and that even in the most painful moments of your life you can feel and then choose again. I am not asking you to bypass pain or your feelings and emotions, what I am suggesting is that when an emotion arises you can see that in that moment you have chosen to feel it. Secondly, you have the power to change it. Anything you resist or judge will remain tightly in place.

What you resist persists.

Only a gentle, kind acknowledgement of what you, the power-keeper have moved towards offers you the opportunity to choose again. Your false principles over time will offer you very little value as you begin to realise happiness is a choice. You will increase your mental health and you will release others from the burden you have placed on them. In your secret inner rule book remember it will state the rules clearly about how people need to be for you to be happy; what they need to say; how you should be treated; how others should be treated; your rule book is so focused on what you need from others you are left never questioning what you can offer yourself. Release your loved ones and the world from your rule book and you will begin to see how there is another world that you have missed altogether. A world of miracles with profound beauty and freedom to feel true deep feelings. Your chains not only hold you captive but the entire world you see is held in the same captivity.

Not so long ago, I was having a conversation with a young, very beautiful woman. She mentioned to me that she only attracts men who are not trustworthy. She said it with a sadness

PRINCIPLE TWO

in her voice, a helplessness. I listened to her story and couldn't help but see how confused she was.

I asked her quietly, 'Do you think it is possible you simply have no idea how to choose the right partner for yourself? Maybe it is not that there is something preventing you from attracting good men, you are just not doing the right homework and taking your time?'

When we are troubled or believe we cannot achieve something we want badly in our lives, it is that the real guidance is missing, there is nothing wrong with us, we simply don't know how. Choosing a life partner has been left to the Disney model of love, how devastating. We all know the one where the princess looks for her prince and instantly they are in love and live happily ever after. Many generations of women have been brainwashed by this ideology but fairy tales once upon a time had a different reason for existing. They were used to help young women transition into womanhood, wiser and stronger. The Disney model changed all that and we were offered a version that had us looking for love outside of ourselves. I spent years trying to find a life partner after my divorce, I still believed I would find the one. I had no idea. I had no idea how to choose, how to discern. Choosing your life partner can take time, it isn't a chemistry thing. You can have a deep connection with a man but this isn't the reason to bond yourself to him for life. Let us teach our young women to get to know men before saying, 'yes'. Disney love doesn't conquer all, it makes a mess of all.

When we think about our lives working, our dreams manifesting, what we need above all else is a healthy state of mind – from here comes a healthy state of heart.

PRINCIPLE TWO

Have you ever considered the question, what are we doing here? I remember the very day when broken and lost I was lying on my bed. As I looked around my room I noticed emptiness everywhere, regardless of the beautiful furnishings and decorations there was a deep profound emptiness in my chest. I asked this very question, 'What am I doing here?' I noticed my breathing was agitated as I felt anger and frustration, I was lost and I didn't like it. My heart beat faster and yet I was following the instructions of my business consultant. Yes, that's right, I reached out looking for help. My new skincare line that I was banking on and was my dream to change everything had fallen apart. A bad business deal had left me in debt owing money to a family member. All of my guilt and shame surfaced in my mind, I was a failure and had invested money from someone I dearly loved and now everything was at risk. I could hardly walk up the stairs of my apartment, my body was aching and my mind constantly reeled with thoughts looking for answers. The stress levels rose and I began to feel an intolerance towards the smallest things, my parenting was not even the first thing on my mind anymore. As I looked at my children, I was miles away, so busy thinking about how to fix our lives that I couldn't even see them. Children know this, they feel it and in their own vulnerability they make up their own false beliefs about why they are not seen and hence the perpetuation of suffering. In this book, I promise you will learn how to reverse this once and for all. My business consultant, who later I discovered had just recently stepped away from running a spiritual community in country Victoria, gave me strict instructions. 'Lie down on your bed and imagine your calves sinking into the mattress.' I thought he had lost his mind.

Here he was, a slick handsome man whose business was working with CEOs of large companies to get them back on track and charging an hourly rate of $350 to $500 an hour was helping me, no fee? That was the first miracle. Why would he do it? I didn't think about it too long, I just said 'yes' and the following three months we were together every day. Destiny was at play. Our first meeting lasted seven hours, where we sat across from each other at a cafe. I listened mesmerised to every word. This was my first real awakening. He spoke about life, beliefs, love, meditation. Part of my mind was thinking, What has this got to do with my business? And yet my heart was pounding, This information is the answer, as I stared, not even really seeing him. I wondered if this was what I had always wanted to know. The cafe was getting busier and yet it felt empty as if we were the only two people in the room. At the beginning of our day, he asked me if I meditated. I almost laughed but I wasn't comfortable enough, so I said a quiet, 'No'. I'm a doer, what good would meditation do? I thought, confused. I began to look around wondering if we had overstayed our welcome in the cafe. Nervously, I began to look at him again and decided that regardless of all of my thoughts about meditation, I would follow his instructions. It felt like everything else I had heard prior was old information and what he was sharing was something I had forgotten but was now remembering.

So there I was lying on my bed and putting all of my attention on my calves, following instructions. I had tried ev-

Dignity is our right when we choose honestly. No one has the power to take it from us, for no matter what is done to us, dignity comes from what we choose and how we choose to move our power.

erything and nothing was working, my life, my dreams, my coping mechanisms and my way of doing life was over. As my attention went to my calves my thoughts increased and so did my frustration. I was sure I was doing it wrong, my thoughts weren't supposed to be increasing and all of my own ideas about meditation surfaced. Again the moment filled with ideas until in desperation I asked for help. My exact words were, 'I have no idea about my life, why I am here? I have no idea if there is something more meaningful out there, I want to know, reveal yourself to me.'

I surrendered and opened a door I had closed for so long. Finally, I had access to a deeper level of mind, heart and being. I had been living from such a superficial level of thinking and had shut out deeper levels of intelligence, wisdom and love. In adopting and living from false principles I had no access to what was real, clear and Loving in me. I had literally closed my heart, the doorway to all the mystery, the joy, the Love, the truth. Not just shut but deadlocked.

The next three months were inspiring, I learnt more about true living than I had in more than thirty-three years. My meditation became my love, the stillness and the quiet offered me peace and then I had to learn how to be rested in my life. This was a completely different adventure and learning. What helped me the most was to understand my first purpose. It gave me somewhere to anchor as I began to reverse the use of my power. It was a slow process and yet along the way I met, loved and found some of this planet's most profound human beings, to learn from and evolve with. I began connecting with my soul family.

PRINCIPLE TWO

I realised I didn't know what I was doing here, life had to have a deeper meaning. Mind you, I wasn't asking haphazardly after all my life was a mess. I had my dreams broken, my marriage was over, I was a single mother. I had just left behind an abusive short relationship and I was heartbroken again. Even though I wanted my old life before this meltdown to work out, I knew deep in my heart it was meaningless, missing something that fulfils beyond things, other people and places. I was empty, looking for meaning in houses, businesses, trying to keep up with the Joneses. My entire existence was about the external world, how others saw me. How hollow. An over-thinker, you know, when your mind doesn't stop and you wake up in the early hours of the morning thinking. I worried about things and often focused on others and what they were doing and how I could change them so I could feel okay. When I think back to my life then, I can only be thankful everything fell apart and with my willingness, I had to start all over again. I didn't know, that is the key here, I was willing to admit I had no idea and that was the perfect code for what was to come.

Humility became my ally and my life became an outpouring of miracles daily. I had the living proof there was more to living than meets the eye. Our self-importance and fear of not being in control stunts our willingness to see what is really before us. I was on a precipice and changing my destiny. My children were innocent as was I. However, all was about to change. They were the most special special, extraordinary little people. I cannot even begin to describe how much they taught me. With my world having fallen apart and all of my ideas of how my life should be looking completely scraped from under me, at times I was depressing.

It was very unusual for me to depress, I was much better at mustering all of my force and determination and changing life to suit me, but this time was different. I couldn't. I had to hit rock bottom and be completely undone. Everything changed.

Experience isn't where we can create change, reality is moving and we can either move with it openheartedly needing nothing to be different or we can shut down and harden. Your experience offers you the opportunity to be with it in either of two ways. You have choice, this is where you as the power-keeper can choose where to anchor your belief in every given moment. You can in your experience anchor yourself in your true nature or you can bring the false you to the table. Each of them will offer you a different outcome. You are choosing this for your life. Do I need to tell you what will offer you the happiness, clarity and life you seek? As the years have begun to fly by, my body now experiences the different sensations of pain, discomfort as it begins to find its new rhythm.

Now in my fifties, it seems as though everything physical is changing. I find myself surprised at what I see in the mirror, wondering what it will be like to have wrinkles I cannot control or change. In my own inner world, I feel like a young girl, playful, full of curiosity and enchanted by the real knowledge I have gained access to during my life. I understand the ancient way of the wise women, revered in times gone by when wisdom mattered more than how we looked in the mirror. Sometimes, when my body is experiencing real discomfort I find myself considering solutions. Is it my hormones? Do I need to exercise more? I begin to watch these thoughts and notice how they draw me deeper into my discomfort. My discomfort becomes a problem. Suddenly I realise I can ask the question in the midst of the flurry of solutions in my mind, is it really a problem? Instantly I feel space of freedom from the experience in my body and I see I have a choice. I draw my attention deep within, where I know all the peace I need exists. My experience is not the sum of what I am and in this, my heart opens. I breathe a little deeper and begin to notice that my peace never left me and I dive in. In this space of openheartedness, I notice my body relax and all that was before, the discomfort, the pain is simply no longer. I am free. A thought arises, it's so easy. My day begins. It isn't really about whether the pain stays or goes, it is simply going deeper in my own mind, not allowing thoughts and feelings to lead me. You are a treasure, remember what you see in the mirror is a mere speck of what you really are. What's really important to remember here is that you are real, but not all ideas are. As it is the very function of illusion to appear real, most likely you will not be able to navigate in this using your conceptual thought, as reasoning and justification are what the reality of illusion relies on. Rather, you need to access that deeper level of choice. The only way to do that cleanly is by placing no trust in your own thoughts and emotions because they will reflect the embedded community of meaning you take to be you. You can't solve a problem from within the problem itself. Trust in thought and feeling

The part of you within your own mind that leans into the true principles of the universe, the part of you that reads them and knows – this part of yourself takes you to a doorway that when opened will give you access to your true nature – Love!

is something that must be earned. It is not inherent as many people tend to believe.

If you feel free and alive when you read The Power Shift, you are recognising truth inside your own mind and heart, you may even have feelings of aliveness. You will feel the truth. Truth cannot be taught, it can only be extended and in the extension where it lands one will respond or react. If you react and get huffy and puffy, don't despair, keep reading, in the midst of the upheaval you are still moving forward.

The ego thought system is founded on the assumption that guilt and shame are meaningful and therefore fear. It will attempt to make you despondent and feel sinful. It is just the way it works. The ego thought system without you is nothing. It doesn't exist. It is in a word, loveless. For some, they may be okay in choosing to live this way, for others their time has come.

When we think about our lives working, our dreams manifesting, what we need above all else is a healthy state of mind – from here comes a healthy state of heart. Without trusting and moving in alignment with true universal principles any correction to our lives is temporary.

This principle has a polar opposite, a voice. This voice is loud and we can find it everywhere, in Hollywood, billboards, the daily news, magazine articles, just to name a few; however, just because we can hear it doesn't mean we need to believe it as true. If your child was doing his homework using a mathematical formula he had constructed by himself and was frustrated because he couldn't solve his math equation, would you berate him? No, you would offer him the correct formula. There is nothing different here, it is your life, your happiness, your mental health, your relationships that are at risk. So what is the false principle here, it sounds a little like others control my happiness, I am not responsible for my inner choices, it was what they did that made me sad, angry. Of course when we read this it sounds awkward, however, we cannot deny our leaning towards justifying the truth of this false principle. Why? Because it is ingrained not only in our own minds but our nervous system. We have chosen it over and over and over so that it is now a very bad habitual reaction. Even if we say, I know I can choose, we don't really believe it yet.

Your life matters, as do the lives of your loved ones and every other human being you get to meet during your lifetime. Reaching out to you with real knowledge and supporting you to live a meaningful and rich life is my deepest wish. Therefore we must investigate and explore together, unlearn, undo and most importantly become accustomed to listening. Side-stepping the loud voices of the old and finding your true inner voice that whispers to you with kindness is a beautiful beginning. This quiet whisper belongs to your true nature, and as we begin to expose the false principle here we will take back our power, gently and lovingly we will begin to change our lives without any external doing.

Remember, "You choose and the entire universe alters."

I have lived so much of my life longing for a higher love and to find my way in this world, not as my parents did or those around me. I wanted more than this. I knew there was

PRINCIPLE TWO

another way. I honestly got much more than I bargained for, my very own awakenings led me to not only uncover my own deeper purpose but to create, build and offer the world the very best part of me. It hasn't been easy unlearning false principles that became the very fabric of my mind.

Our second true principle in itself can be mind-altering and confusing, after all for decades in some cases we have lived fully engaged in the belief we are the effect of that which is outside of us. A level of powerlessness and helplessness fuelling our minds and our hearts, triggering our nervous system to react and project outwardly.

The true principles shared here give you the golden key, each principle has a secret code you can remember as you begin unlocking doors and take new and happier pathways in your life.

Dignity is our right when we choose honestly. No one has the power to take it from us, for no matter what is done to us, dignity comes from what we choose and how we choose to move our power.

Through the doorway you see differently, you are no longer looking for what needs fixing or flaws in others, you begin to experience a new vision, as if the fog has been wiped away. As the power-keeper, you happily accept a new level of responsibility. After all, you now know how to be happy, open, curious, loving.

As you begin to accept and experience the power of principle two, you love knowing there is no one else making your inner choices for your happiness and success. True happiness and success rise from your inner world. You decide. How we react to our experiences is our choice, we are moving power according to our beliefs. The exciting part being we see all that is standing between us and choose happiness in our lives, even when others are acting badly and we are not getting what we want. When we fully recognise we choose our stress and unhappiness from within our minds and that we are the mechanism of choice, we begin to open ourselves up to a happier and more meaningful life. Many of our struggles disappear into thin air and we begin to enjoy the ability we have to move our power and have the wisdom to use it appropriately. We will be more available for our loved ones, more curious and kinder.

For some they experience an awakening to their true nature spontaneously. Our world often embraces these awakened beings, revering them and their knowledge. I have experienced a number of awakenings, all of them deeply undoing. To awaken and stay this way is a deep choice. I have loved learning and getting to choose. My way has been to bring a deep kindness to my world, seeing how resistance and judgement of oneself is merely a part of the cycle of living by false principles. Awakenings come in all forms and even the subtlest, such as reading this book, support us as we listen for the murmur of truth, the aliveness in our cells telling us that everything is good. What you do with this is your choice, but know one thing, you are the one who chooses and you are the one who holds your joy, your passion, your beauty in your hands, not on the outside but in your mind and heart. To know we have this power initially frightens us and often we feel unworthy as the old ways of thinking rise up. Throughout this book, we learn how to know what voice to heed and which to rest upon.

PRINCIPLE TWO

We will become mothers, wives, lovers, entrepreneurs in the truest sense of these words. We will understand how to be with our emotions without acting on our pain and in our hurt, how to transform all of this misplaced power and divinity. We will be the women we respect and reclaim our dignity as we learn how to move power honestly.

For the very best part of my life, I lived allied with fear. I learned early on to believe in what I was seeing and feeling. I began to lose touch with my inner life, where another voice, gentle, soft and loving, spoke to me and the voices of the world became loud and I found myself drowning out the voice of Love within me. The world around me became the thing I needed to conquer and to survive. I began to accept the voice of lower mind and built so many walls and false ideas. I built a lower self. The moment it became clear to me that I built the walls, I felt this deep freedom within every cell in my body. My next thought was, If I built them, I can take them down. Here is a great question for you. If the walls we build within us don't protect us from being hurt by others, why do we hold onto them? What was their original purpose and are these illusionary walls actually doing what we set out for them to do? If so, we would have to be the happiest beings in the universe, so why are we so unfulfilled, overwhelmed and unhappy? If you don't ask these tough questions and open your mind, who will?

Understanding why you built these walls – which appear as belief structures, so they aren't walls at all, just energy – is very easy, you don't need years of therapy to get to the bottom of it all. When we resist hurt and pain we turn our back on our infinite unlimited power to open to anything that life has to offer us. We are not restricted by our circumstances just by our willingness to feel and allow. If we truly knew what this did to our inner sacred world we would beg to go back and feel that initial hurt and start again, but right now it all seems reasonable because we don't get it.

When we turn our back on the hurt, which by the way is a normal human feeling, we need to suppress it and replace it with another more palatable emotion, such as anger, bitterness, resentment, depression, we need to do something other than let that hurt into our heart and feel broken. Did you know when hurt breaks your heart you are saying yes to more of your own innocence and purity? How many times did you shut your heart down and resist being hurt, can you remember? Undoubtedly, each time you take a step further into your dark place in your heart, fear opens its arms and welcomes you into its lair. Harsh. So is believing that you have to close your heart and sacred world to avoid pain. You are the perfection of the universe and infinite energy, so how can you truly believe that you cannot open your heart to hurt? How long do wish to remain under the spell of this false belief and for how many generations will you demonstrate this falseness?

Let's be frank, even though you have put up all these incredible coping mechanisms to avoid feeling hurt, have they worked? Do you at times feel anxious, separate, alone, fearful, unable to achieve your potential, a failure as a parent, wife, lover? If you said yes to even one of the above, it is your coping mechanisms to avoid hurt that are making you miserable. Life isn't going to change, I guarantee you and nor is reality unless you do. The only alternative for happiness, joy, dignity and respect is a power shift.

When you engage in conversations, interactions with almost 99% of the people in your life, more often than not you are reaching their own filters they have set up to protect themselves from experiencing hurt and pain. When you say yes over and over to false principles, you close your heart to the magic that is alive and thriving beyond all filters.

Fear breeds fear. The self you built on false principles is flawed, you know this now and yet you have built our own inner reality based on its ideology. You have put it at the helm of your life and wonder why you are in difficulty. Fear is in charge of your happiness, fulfilment and peace. Its principle is to place the responsibility of how it feels externally. In fact, it cannot take responsibility for how it is experiencing its life because it would then have to admit to its flawed existence. To begin power shifting you need to accept this self you have built and how it keeps you bound, enslaved to a false sense of reality. To a belief in guilt, shame and blame; they are the rules of the game you play when you say yes to it.

The part of you within your own mind that leans into the true principles of the universe, the part of you that reads them and knows – this part of yourself takes you to a doorway that when opened will give you access to your true nature – Love! Beauty of undeniable magnitude.

Love has no opposite. When you enter you will not find fear.
Fear or lack cannot enter.

Getting to know fear and seeing the purpose it serves in your life is helpful. The reason for this is that you get to see fear has no real power.

PRINCIPLE TWO

Love at this level cannot be compromised or threatened.

I remember when everything fell apart. I had some of the most beautiful, intelligent and awakened people enter my life. I looked up to them. I remember thinking I wasn't as good as them, if only they knew the thoughts I had, the fears, the anxieties, the things I had done. I was plagued by these thoughts and the more I reversed my beliefs the stronger my thoughts became. All I had was willingness, that's it. A willingness to live my life differently.

I remember driving home after a recent break up with a man I had a very strong connection to. I was devastated when he told me our love was too much, he was afraid he would disappear if he embraced it, so he had to leave. Those words rang in my ears for hours, I was in shock. Why would you want to walk away from that? I wondered in my suffering. I simply couldn't understand.

In hindsight and with my newfound wisdom, years later I can now see that as beautiful as he was and how strong our connection, he was so mixed up and confused but there I was, the saviour. Over the years I learnt from my mentor and teacher that when choosing a life partner you must do your homework. I loved hearing him speak about this, I loved how romance had nothing to do with selecting a life partner. If romance, chemistry, a strong connection, physical attraction come first, we can be deluded and lose track of what matters most. Love and romance come in bucket loads when you choose well. Here again, Disney love is often our guide. Choosing a life partner isn't a game and it cannot be handed across to Hollywood and the romantic movies we love so much. If I had done my homework I would have valued the connection but not stepped into a relationship, but back in those days I was a novice and I made so many mistakes. Nothing is lost and in this case, it was dearly true.

So there I was in the driver seat, my dear friend Jenny in the passenger seat and my two darlings in the back seat, not fighting, that was a joy. It was far too dark for them to fight, they were tired, and as I was driving I became lost in my thoughts about the day, the sadness breaking my heart, I opened and opened to it. The silence in the car was deafening and as I quietly I was being broken, as a deep and expansive Love began to move through me, my mind immediately thought, this is my love for Mark, giving it away just like that. Quietly another voice could be heard, it was a voice I had grown to love, so gently it said, this Love is you. The entire car was filled with this divine Love. As we entered the driveway we all walked to the front verandah, I had my keys in my hand, not a word was spoken. We were in the dark as the porch light remained off. I opened the door and once again as I walked to switch on the light I felt arms around me and there she was my little girl, 'Mum, I love you.' Children know Love, their filters still not solidified and hardened.

This experience changed my life, it was like a miracle leaving me with new knowledge and wisdom. It was a year later when I began to really understand what had happened

PRINCIPLE TWO

that night and how an experience that seemed devastating became a golden gem.

We have learned to project love outwardly, rather than own it as our nature – we felt it because of another, nature may open us to feel love, something external – in reality, this is not so. We experience it because we know it and we are that.

Imagine if you decided to reverse the idea in your mind for the need of love with the idea that you, as Love, get to extend it to your world. It may be a kind word to the lady at the grocery counter, the butcher when buying your lamb chops, or a gentle ear when your child is angry seeing beyond the anger and reaching them. Suddenly, you are in a new space.
You see, it is after all, all about you.

If you were to believe this above all else you would experience the full power of belief, you would also stop believing all the beliefs telling you this isn't so.

To need love is to seek something that in reality, is not outside of you. It is one of the greatest myths and when we do not question it, it limits our entire reality.

In the words of Ramana Maharishi, arguably the most revered Indian sage of the twentieth century: 'The mind is a bundle of thoughts. The thoughts arise because there is a thinker. The thinker is the ego. The ego, if sought, will automatically vanish.'

The thought, "I need love" is a false belief. Left unexamined, we will die never knowing the joy of our true identity. Our belief in this one thought, that "we need love" to be happy, means we will be moving our power dishonestly. Remember, our false use of our power shuts us down, not just our heart but our everything. Our thinking becomes limited, our abilities as the infinite source of energy that we are will not come to fruition. It is a lot to give up for one pesky belief, so why do we not want to give it up. Why do you want to hold on to a belief, and base your entire life of false principles inviting in fear and lack?

In our subconscious mind, we know what Love is, in fact, I will go so far as to say in our subconscious we know everything, we know the whole truth. To go against what we know in this way is the greatest suffering so we suppress it and make up a false reality based on false beliefs and principles, projecting our false needs and wants onto a world that will never, ever be able to offer them to us.

The Disney model is wrong and it will never offer you the deep love you long for, it will look a little like what our children are facing right now. We have never before seen such an increase in suicide and depression, our children drugged because they have no idea how to be happy. Our children are not mentally unwell, they are suffering from a lack of real knowledge to live a fulfilling and happy life. We cannot teach them by telling them, only by demonstrating what is true and allow them to find their way back to us and to their own hearts when they choose. Control, worry and manipulative micro-managing will only cause them more confusion and divide their minds. They will feel weak and unable to navigate through life when they have all the power to do so magnificently.

When we accept the part within our own minds still trying to live our life from immature love, Disney love, we will see also that this immature part of our mind when given our power leaves us believing we are weak, afraid, over controlling

PRINCIPLE TWO

and domineering. Either way, we are not fulfilled in our hearts. Feeling anger, fear, despondency and isolated from our true nature are the consequence of our choosing this immature path. It need not remain this way, there is another way.

Real Love does not have an opposite, it is just like a dark room as you walk in and switch on the light, the darkness is no longer real. It has no reality.

What we are is the very essence of the universe, an unlimited resource of energy. We in our truest essence are the holders of such immense power and yet we know little of this and offer what we do know to the false misunderstandings of a child. As we anchor our mind in false principles we are experiencing the outcomes of such beliefs.

There are a number of reasons why people look for deeper meaning in their lives. Someone is in deep suffering due to an external circumstance or inner conflict or depression. A person is looking for a better life to achieve new goals. A person wants more intimacy, sees their weaknesses and wants to evolve, to grow. To become a better person, a good person. And of course, we have the spontaneous awakening.

It doesn't matter why we look, the reasons can affect what we find and how deeply we seek real change. For those who wish to use deeper meaning to achieve goals and success only as the key driver behind their efforts, they may find themselves confronted by the need for deep honesty when facing their inner world. Others who are suffering an inner conflict may welcome the honesty and dig deeper and evolve powerfully. There are different levels of searching for answers to the question we have about our lives.

The Power Shift

When we begin to recognise our error, we become driven by a quest to find the true meaning of Love above all else. It's so simple really. It isn't about becoming spiritual or changing your career or your life. For parents, this is a gift for your children and their children, for wives and husbands, awaits a deeper intimacy and bond, for all others, there is the opportunity to find meaning in all things big or small, and delight in true principles and codes that will unlock the magic of the universe.

You are not only what you see with your physical eyes, your inner world is immense and without boundaries and limits. It is the intelligence of the universe that keeps us from seeing all that we are, we couldn't withstand its magnificence and its magnitude when we are anchored in small-mindedness and immature patterns. However, with a new level of responsibility and honesty, we have access to glimpses of this beauty, one tiny glimpse at a time.

Our seeing with our physical eyes is so limited and therefore so is our belief. We see what we believe and we believe what we see. Our world is limited only by this, as is science and the exploration of the universe. Quantum physics has begun to offer us more and for many of us, it is a comfort to accept science and physics. At some point, when you directly can access your true nature you will not need confirmation from the outside, for now, it may be helpful.

The difference between direct knowledge and second-hand knowledge is worlds apart. We will throughout our time together explore what direct knowledge is revealing to us and of course allowing us to see the false. From this per-

PRINCIPLE TWO

fect place, we can begin to undo that which we have adopted without investigation or inquiry and what we directly know the truth of.

Imagine for a moment, if the universe, what you are, is far beyond anything you currently can see and feel. Your body a mere idea in your mind and only because you see and feel it becomes such a strong belief. It takes up so much of your attention. Now, imagine a blind person who cannot see their body but they can feel, they are blessed with the need to access what is subtler, the space around them means more to them, they are not bound by their physical eyes. Our physical reality need not bind us into smallness, we use it for its true purpose, to evolve, to unify and to unlock the doorway we closed so long ago to our true nature, here whilst we are in a body.

Those who still have access to their true nature and seek to allow more of it into their lives, walk many paths in this world, they are intellectuals, academics, architects, doctors, highly successful business people, both men and women, IT geniuses, musical geniuses, authors, yoga instructors, construction workers, retirees, artists, teenagers, teachers, miners, children, mothers, fathers, grandmothers, grandfathers.

There is no limit and no restrictions when your heart calls, it's time. Our time here isn't about what we see with our physical eyes. This is only a surface level of understanding and seeing. Its limitation is similar to how little of our brain we use. Our physical sight is the same it shows us so little and yet we believe, mostly that is all that there is. How wrong we are.

If we continue to believe love is something we need to get externally, whether it comes as acceptance, appreciation, being taken care of by others, we all define the meaning that we attach to love, we are anchored in what is false. That belief in the false idea of our life is enough to frighten us and distort our life flow. We distort ourselves in the hope that we can find the missing piece. When all along this love we are seeking is an illusion and is the mythical love of Disney movies and fairy tales.

Getting to know fear and seeing the purpose it serves in your life is helpful. The reason for this is that you get to see fear has no real power. Anyone that tells you to beat fear or speaks about fear as an enemy is wrong. Fear has no power over you. You are an infinite source of unlimited energy, how can fear have the power to control you. You can choose fear if you wish and the only reason we choose anything is because we believe it has a purpose and serves to fulfil one of our goals. Even though, right now, you cannot accept this and when anxiety and fear arise you believe you are at the effect of this outside force and power, I am here to tell you, look again.

What fear serves in my world is to limit me, anchoring me in what is false and opening up pathways that are deluded and untrue. Fear rises up to support our internal anchoring. You will hear the voices of your own internal anchoring. What port have you dropped the anchor into? Is it the port of immature love or mature love. Wherever you said yes, that is what voices you will hear. However, all is not lost, Love awaits silently for your tiny little bit of willingness. Here is where the mature part of you gets to take control, meaningful control, not of others but of your own internal anchoring by asking, 'What do I want right now?' If you want fear you can have

PRINCIPLE TWO

it, it will make you right and you may even feel powerful and in control, one thing is for certain, you will separate yourself from yourself and others. Fear knows no unity, it knows and speaks only of separation. If this is what you want to accept it, go for it, if it isn't you will lay down the sword and ask for help from the part of you within that is your eternal servant waiting for you to call upon it. You have access to the part of you within that knows how to live your life, the Lover within you whose language is oneness, joy, peace, true strength. Fear will tell you that Love is weak, this is a lie, only what we fear makes us weak, Love is beyond weakness it is the source of all things, it is all powerful, it is you.

Fear has a language we must wise up to, the more you recognise it, the more choice you will have. When you want to be right, fear will be there whispering in your ear that you should fight on, there is justification in your behaviour. It will whisper the language of fear which is separation. Guilt and shame have no place in this reversal, as they too are fear speaking.

The saying, 'fear breeds contempt' is spot on.

Look at it this way, if you were living out your life with true principles at the helm of your ship fear wouldn't be needed. Your anchor would be dropped into the sea of Love. So, it isn't the fear that you need to be concerned about but rather go deeper and look at what you need the fear for. Fear is merely a useful tool that keeps false principles alive and thriving. So, when anyone keeps you focused on eliminating it to help solve your problems, they are wrong. Ask again, 'What is the purpose fear is serving in this moment for me?'

Every thought you think has a level of vibrational energy. Untouched and without you assigning it a purpose, this thought will arise and it will disappear, no matter how dark it is.

PRINCIPLE TWO

Now we can see that fear is a powerful tool in recognising when we are anchored in a false principle. All things can be used for goodness or to reinforce the false, isn't this amazing? When we recognise anxiety or fearful thoughts arising, we can simply know we are anchored in a false principle, that's it, just in recognising this you will feel instant relief. Sit quietly and allow your thoughts to be seen but no judged, offer yourself the opportunity to become the observer of your thoughts. You will see the path they are taking, the road they are taking you down and you can decide right now if that is what you want.

All of the tools and principles offered here will give you a tiny glimpse of what you have always wanted over your current life, as you gently and kindly begin to explore what is possible. You are in control of your giving, this includes the giving of your power, one of the most important gifts a human being possesses.

I am going to challenging you a little now. In your current state, you see fear as the polar opposite of Love. You may even believe if you are experiencing fear that you cannot know Love at the same time. However, this isn't true. Love is like a container, you are like a container and
you can hold everything. Here we will undo fear and begin to see what it serves. I want you to see that you are the master of fear, it isn't the other way around. Fear is mastered by you.

Fear is a tool used by our anchoring in what is false within our own minds. If we were in the jungle and being chased by a lion, fear is a survival mechanism that we are genetically programmed to experience and has its purpose, however, this isn't the fear we are speaking about. Emotional fear limits us like a child with monsters under its bed. Monsters under our bed terrify us into believing there is something and it can hurt me, it is bigger and stronger than me and it is mean and evil. How does a child reconcile this fear of being at the mercy of something evil? As parents, we turn on the light and hug our child and in time we look under the bed together to reveal the misunderstanding. The child was wrong. The monster is not there. However, the idea of the darkness harbouring fearful creatures remains in the child's subconscious. Have you ever considered what purpose fear serves, why we choose it over and over and over again? Have you ever considered why you chose it in the first place and make it an ally, make it real? Even grasping this new idea may be confronting. I know right now you may believe that fear isn't your choice and you are at the effect of it. This is totally understandable. However, I am here to tell you over and over, fear is not bigger than you and when you stop needing it to offer you the purpose you have given, it will quietly recede back to nothingness.

Over the last twenty years, I have supported and offered my mentorship to hundreds of students, in one capacity or another, extending the opportunity to see the mechanisms we use to stay anchored in our false principles. When I worked as a workshop author and facilitator, empowering women with serious conditions such as anorexia, bulimia, divorce and other challenges, my life was rewarded through the anchoring of myself in what was deepest within me. Now, as a principal trainer for Brow Secrets™ International, I am once again offering what I know to hundreds of my students as they begin building lives they love. What I have noticed more than anything else during this time is we ask the wrong questions. When you are anchored in your false principles don't expect to ask the right questions.

Everything in your life when you are alert offers insight into your own inner anchoring. Fear, as we mentioned and continue to see, is an example of this. Fear cannot appear without cause. The cause is in your mind, to begin with as is everything. Asking the right questions is a great practice, giving you the opportunity to choose once again in any given moment. You can with the right questions be enraged and immediately withdraw all of your power from the rage and in that moment, you may change the destiny of your life. You may be depressing and once again with the right questions, you shift your power. Accepting that you have this choice at any given moment is one of the most significant realisations you can have in your life. It is life changing.

The moment emotional fear is made real, you can say we have caused a split inside of our own heart and mind. There is fear and there is also something else we really want; Love, acceptance, respect, abundance, power, just to name a few. However, after this first moment, we rarely, if ever go back to facing the purpose we enlisted fear in the first place as one of our companions. Ultimately, it doesn't matter, it is important to see choosing fear had a purpose at one point in time and it is that purpose that we repeat over and over, even when it doesn't give us what we really want. As we repeat this pattern we reinforce weakness in our mind.

As parents, we see our role is to tell our children they are fantastic and have so much potential in the hope that one day

Worry is another version of fear. Living with fear is not living at all. The simplest way to know when you have fallen off the cart is when you are no longer at peace.

they will recognise this and be free of their own limitations. Conversely, a child needs more than words and encouragement. This is important, she doesn't need a perfect parent or even perfect love, so to beat yourself up for not offering her this is merely once again you anchored in your false principles. What she does need is a parent with humility and the willingness to reverse the need for false principles and give her power to what is true. A child recognises this willingness immediately and in this, she learns to love herself regardless of her misunderstandings, she opens up to the real purpose of her life and begins to love learning her true purpose, forgiveness Love, kindness, compassion, understanding. You have only one task as a parent – to demonstrate your willingness to make your life about your highest purpose first – this gift for a child is gold.

Over time, we lose sight of our highest purpose and we attempt to build lives from our wants and needs. We teach our children that things will one day make them happy and their security is found in what they will one day build and own. We teach them that love is found outside of them and we show them this each moment we choose fear over Love. We rarely, if ever go back to facing the purpose we enlisted fear in the first place as one of our companions. Ultimately, it is important to see choosing fear had a purpose at one point, and it is that purpose that we repeat over and over and over, even when it separates us from what we really want.

What precedes fear is what matters, fear itself is like a shovel you use to dig a hole, why are you digging the hole in the first place, do you have a purpose? Fear can come through repeatedly as a powerful emotional pattern in our body. We feel it and we contract, we want to be rid of it, we are even afraid of it. Is that crazy or what? All of these ideas that you just read happen in your mind. Unless there is a lion chasing you down the street, this use of your mind is you using intelligence to create fantasies of fear and separation. We are so intelligent, as a species, we learn early on how to use our own minds to build a false reality. A reality that frightens us and keeps us tied to our one goal – mastering our most hurtful moment as a child.

You will come to know this belief holds you bound to the re-creation of the same painful story it arose from. It may look different, the people may be different, however, what you are trying to master is still the same. When you see this and recognise the pain it causes you, you will also see that it is a fruitless task and you cannot master a false reality, a false problem you created in the first place. Living out this illusion is our greatest misunderstanding. To sustain this illusion you need many tools, fear, false principles and the misuse of your power. It is a sad, sad, story.

Fear will speak a thousand words and those words will be exactly what you need to hear to keep you stuck and unhappy, continually seeking to externalise the solution to an inside problem. We use it just the same way a drug addict uses cocaine as a tool to achieve a goal. You use fear to bind you to your false principles which rise from the idea that your happiness and your value exists outside of you.

Our physical senses tell us that we are separate and therefore we have our minds and our thoughts which we are responsible for. It tells us we have done bad things and we deserve the bad things that happen to us and we must repent. These false principles we anchor our experience to offer us infinite flavours of separation and suffering. Supporting an idea in our mind that the monster under our bed is now outside of us and we must fight to survive. Our lives become about avoiding what we fear and grasping for what we believe we need. Turn around take a look within.

Love answers everyone.

In my personal experience, this is wholly true. Love is within our minds, we mentioned this earlier when I suggested to you that your subconscious mind knows everything, including the truth about everything. Isn't it amazing to even consider? There is a part of your mind that has access to the most ancient wisdom. It also stores all of your memories, absolutely everything.

To begin unravelling the massive labyrinth we have built over time of our feelings of dissatisfaction, striving, overwhelm, unhappiness, hate and fear we must want to see honestly. We have to take a moment, to know what is in the darkness and what has kept us so afraid for so long. We don't need to unravel our false principles, but consider what truly matters, how do we be with the thoughts that arise, our emotions our feelings. We can begin to see belief is the key to moving power and we must learn how to move it honestly. When you place belief in what is false you must accept the false principles you become bound to. One cannot exist without the other. When you stop anchoring yourself in a false belief you can no longer find any purpose for the false principles you would need to uphold this belief. Everything false crumbles and only what is true can remain. Your power automatically shifts. When you choose to believe in a false belief you have one purpose and one purpose only which is to separate yourself from your true nature.

As you seek out your true nature and begin to find bits and pieces of it throughout your day, for example, you may find a deep inner rest while working, a stillness within even when your world feels a little chaotic, joy rising up for no good reason. Your life will become sweeter, kinder. So, what does that mean? For some, this may be a little esoteric or just plain crazy. For others believing all we are is just a physical body which lives for some time and then is gone, dead, you may be disappointed with what you will find here. However, here is your challenge, if your beliefs are steadfast, what possibly could be threatened for you to examine them? Try this next part of this book on for size, you may even like to notice what it threatens inside of you if you were to open and questioned your current beliefs. I will not mess around with ways to reach you. You are old enough to know and also old enough to turn away. You would agree nothing is threatened as you are the power-keeper, you choose where you travel within. I have no power over you or what you will ultimately decide, nobody does.

As you begin to see the power of your beliefs you will want to examine them. When you feel fearful, restless, angry, find yourself depressing or tuning into negative emotions and thoughts in your mind you now have a practical intervention. You can and will most probably forget you have this choice,

PRINCIPLE TWO

however, for the times, you remember you will be able to consider where you are anchored and what belief you are holding onto that is no longer serving your new life. What you want now may be very different to what a girl needed when she was four years old.

When you let an old belief unravel, let it go and release it, it may very well feel as though a part of you that you have identified with is dying. When core beliefs are dissolving it can feel devastating. However, you will survive to find you no longer need what holds no true value to the life you now wish to live. You are not dying, just like the caterpillar isn't, simply transforming into a beautiful new species. You will see new abilities enter your mind and you may with continual honesty feel the magic of the power shift. Love, after all, is what you are. A frequency so pure and so meaningful, to know it is to be devoted to it with all of your heart and soul. Love has never left you and will never desert you.

Fear will give us all the adrenaline we need to escape a truly dangerous situation. It is useful; nonetheless, fear that is releasing these fight and flight chemicals over and over again where there is simply no danger is the cause of widespread mental health issues and physical sickness. The purpose of fear is to continually reinforce your smallness, lack and to reinforce in your mind that you need to continue believing your survival and happiness depend on false principles. Let's explore some more reasons fear arises: lack of money; getting old; never finding love; an illness; a child not being safe; a failing business; feeling overweight; feeling too skinny; feeling alone, even the planet warming. We could write a book on

Living a life asleep means that you have unexamined, unquestioned beliefs, beliefs that perpetuate the way you move your power through the choices you make.

PRINCIPLE TWO

the justified reasons why we should be afraid. This type of addiction allies you with lower vibrations of thought. Worrying about what could happen becomes a part of everyday life and also something you use to feel in control. Every thought you think has a level of vibrational energy. Untouched and without you assigning it a purpose, this thought will arise and it will disappear, no matter how dark it is. The next time you want to give your time over to thoughts about other people and these thoughts are negative, hateful, no matter how justified in your own mind, think again. You are pouring your power into the negativity of it, attracting and beckoning lower energies to attach themselves to you and tempt you and sadly the consequences will befall you. Thoughts have no power. Beliefs beckon your power. Choice is where the power shift comes in.

PRINCIPLE THREE

False Principle
My happiness and inner peace are dependent on my ability to control life and other people.

True Principle
It is only by looking honestly at the manner in which I engage and move power within myself that I am able to change my destiny, deepen my relationships and live fully.

Let me share a personal story with you. During the past twenty years, I have had the honour of meeting, spending time with and learning from some of the world's most awakened beings. The story I am about to tell is about a teacher whose simple practice helped me see worry for what it truly was – an illusion. During a time when my children had grown up enough to venture out into the world with friends, I often worried about them getting hurt. When they were out I just couldn't relax or sleep, I found myself agitated and my mind was in overdrive. I knew this couldn't possibly continue and that there was something I wasn't seeing. Worry was a huge part of how my mother dealt with life. Even though as a child I could see it wasn't a true way and I was an avid learner, whether we like it or not we are destined to repeat patterns, whether they serve us or not. We also are now seeing we have the power to reverse them.

Through my inner transformation, I adopted a number of practices that helped me when I found myself in trouble. Not externally but in my mind where trouble always begins. I began to see and understand worrying was in no way keeping my children safe, but rather leaving me exhausted and pumping stress chemicals through my body which would ultimately make me sick (which was happening). My poor adrenals were spent. I noticed how worry made me feel in control. I was at least doing something, one of which was giving away my happiness and peace. I began to see when I released the need to worry I was very available if anything was ever to happen. I would be ready to take action and worry was never going to change the outcome.

This all sounds so simple, but to a person who is addicted through the continuous use of worry, it wasn't so easy. I really needed to see how futile worry was before I was able to release it. From this time on, my worrisome thoughts continued and I simply had no further purpose for them. They would rise up and I would not judge them, fear them or try to stop them. I simply didn't offer them my power. If I was to resist them, want them gone, I would once again be giving power to them, so I fuelled the power source. Giving power to resistance is part of this cycle of the false. They were no longer useful to me and therefore over time they stopped rising up in my mind. It was and always is a case of attention deficit.

I also noticed during this time that I was following false principles. Not only do I know what is right for me, but I knew what was right for everyone else. Eventually, I was able to see I was making myself sick and I had a choice to be happy. Last but not least, if I thought I could control my children, they proved to me I couldn't. They didn't need to be controlled, they yearned to be loved. Without questioning the beliefs that disturb our peace we will never, ever be free to access our inner peace and joy, clarity and Love. Who do you think would be more powerful and know how to deal with a serious situation, a person shut down from their inner wisdom or a person relaxed and able to take immediate and perfect action? A woman whose clarity, heart and mind is open and functioning at her highest frequency is a powerful woman, she is heartfelt and strong.

Worry is another version of fear. Living with fear is not living at all. The simplest way to know when you have fallen off the cart is when you are no longer at peace.

It can be hard to admit even to ourselves that we are addicted to beliefs we haven't investigated or examined, be-

PRINCIPLE THREE

liefs that inevitably have us using tools such as fear to stay anchored in the false principles they are bound to. False principles when we are totally lost in them can create a sense of drama and excitement, something to talk about at dinner, over social media and to obsess about when we are alone. Mental health is never taught in schools. This is not some deep and profound realisation, just life's curriculum.

The Power Shift is most meaningful in our intimate relationships because it is here our inner beliefs are most visible. When we get past go and we decide a power shift is our higher calling we see opportunity everywhere. You step into your higher calling when you adopt principles that support the highest purpose in your life. Life becomes an adventure, you step away from coping and become familiar with your own power.

Relationships are often our biggest nemesis, we love them when they are going our way and often resent them when we are not getting what we want from them. We take our rule books based on false principles into our relationship and try to build our lives with our significant other. It is like giving your most important relationship to the part of you anchored in false principles. The chances are slim and divorce stats prove this.

You have an entire list of expectations in your rule book and these expectations must be projected onto your partner or husband, we all do this until we learn another way. It's simple to uncover our rules in our rule book, just look for those recurring pain points. The same issue that comes up over and over you cannot resolve. These expectations will always leave you feeling unfulfilled and project your fulfilment onto them.

The pain: My husband isn't supporting me in my willingness to grow.

Belief: Husbands are supposed to support their wives when they want to grow.

The trickery here is that the expectation sounds totally reasonable, your friends would all agree with you and therefore compel you to offer all of your precious power to this expectation. They may see this as taking care of you, loving you. I ask you, is it? You may even have thoughts about finding a better husband who will support you in your growth. This is not uncommon. However, the power you are pouring into this expectation is draining you because essentially you are believing a thought that is completely and utterly false. The belief that husbands should support their wives when they want to grow isn't universal law, therefore it is untrue. We are not talking about what feels better here but the truth. Universal law, code cannot be manipulated, its incorruptible nature is what always remains.

Life doesn't lie. What we have is what we need to make the shift. If you have a husband, boyfriend, lover who isn't supporting you, that's a perfect opportunity. These expectations we have of our partners are the same we expected as a

PRINCIPLE THREE

child, the same perfect love from a parent unable to give. The child not wanting to feel the hurt finds another way, anything rather than feeling the hurt. This is how one true feeling becomes a series of emotions, energy moving outwardly instead of moving inwardly. It becomes anger, bitterness, resentment, depression and a big story normally accompanies it. When this hurt is allowed to move inwardly, and yes, it may feel uncomfortable, it will travel through unencumbered and leave, a beautiful clean letting go. When it is projected outwardly it will contort your inner world and will contract around this energy. This energetic knot will be triggered over and over until one day you open and release the energy, allowing an old hurt to finally be felt fully. It is this allowance, this willingness to feel reality no matter what form it comes as, grief, betrayal, sadness, that offers us an opportunity to live a more real life. Deeper more intimate relationships, more productivity, clarity, energy.

What we have is what we need to make a power shift. Some worldly experiences can seem far too harsh for such a statement to be believed by us.

Before my brother died, he lived for eleven torturous days with third-degree burns to 75% of his body and my family was broken. I turned to the empty, dark part of my mind and believed love was gone. Feeling my own pain didn't feel like an option. In fact, I focused my attention on my father in the hope that I could help him as he was broken and despondent. I had to do something.

The Power Shift

As a young girl, I remember my mother sharing the story of her lost son over and over and over again. It didn't matter who she met, that was her introduction and each time I watched her my heart broke. The tragedy had become her identity, she was a mother who had lost a son and she lived this out almost until the day she passed. At times I felt angry at her for sharing her tragedy, I couldn't understand why she would do this and I closed my heart, finding the pain unbearable. I didn't close my heart to her, I closed my heart full stop. Now I know the pain is never too much or too unbearable, nevertheless for so long I simply closed my heart and created a pattern. Even when I wished I hadn't I would react and feel the pain of a closed heart. The pain of closing my heart was more unbearable than the pain I wanted to protect myself from. The game was over. How many decades did this take? It seemed like an eternity.

My mother closed her heart and she blamed others for her son's loss, and of course, she blamed herself and she suffered. She may not have known that she had a choice, a choice to feel the devastating pain, to allow it to move through and not to touch even a speck of it. You see if we look a little closer we label energy and then decide why we shouldn't feel it.

To open is to have the willingness to feel everything and know you will survive. Maybe she decided to punish herself, but regardless she too had a choice and she made it. All of her power was poured into the blame, guilt and shame game. She was an extraordinary woman and yet the best version of her was not realised here. I wished my mother was different for decades, I wished she was happier, stronger, more open.

PRINCIPLE THREE

I was living from a false principle and my power was given to this. We cannot change what we decided once upon a time to believe, however, we can pull out the power source and choose again. We can in any given moment decide to turn away from the stories and listen to a kind and gentle voice within. A voice which includes everything and everyone, always.

Our tragedies can be seen as the opportunity to make a power shift, otherwise, they become our stories and we are defined by them. This is the choice we have, the only choice.

It is true that the majority of human beings live their life asleep. Living a life asleep means that you have unexamined, unquestioned beliefs, beliefs that perpetuate the way you move your power through the choices you make. If you are sleeping it would mean that you simply don't question, you just keep moving forward believing you are helpless. Bad habits such as gossip, criticism, blaming and jealousy are common here. If you don't enquire into the beliefs, you are bound and this will limit your potential and your own ability to be intimate with life.

When we don't question and examine our beliefs that cause us pain and instead look externally to fix a problem that really has its core in our own beliefs, we are like machines. Repeating the same over and over, trying to solve the unsolvable puzzle. A little like Groundhog Day – great movie by the way. Nothing is solvable externally in reality. You must have the willingness to step out of the machine-like mechanism and use your intelligence and your wisdom as you travel back to where the seed of your pain is coming from - your own beliefs.

You will feel at the effect of the world and others when in fact the opposite is absolutely true. You can determine the future of the machine mechanism, otherwise, history wouldn't continue to repeat itself. It's that simple. It isn't about changing your behaviour. Let's get that straight. It's about going right to the core and changing the true cause of the issues you face, your own beliefs.

The part of you that finds comfort in the machine mechanism will never question its settings. The part of you suffering, in pain, unable to achieve your potential will. I am speaking to this part of you. Your false principles vibrate at low density so as you can imagine they attract what is lower rather higher. The lower the vibration the more loveless and negative thoughts arise. You have the power to find the core seed and reverse this. As the power-keeper, you can choose to give your power to the superficial level of thinking every moment of your precious life. All addictions begin in the same place, your mind. You cannot shift without belief preceding everything, in fact, belief becomes you. All addictions can be eliminated when the root seed is acknowledged and reversed. Will you need to feel everything your false beliefs stopped you from feeling? The drug addict feels emptiness gnawing in her heart, an alcoholic feels loss or failure, the anorexic and bulimic has feelings of helplessness and guilt, the bully feelings of weakness, last but not least our addiction to food masking the feeling of emptiness or seeming lack of love. Our

Each of us holds the key to ending war on this planet, but first, we must begin by accepting our ability to feel.

The Power Shift

addictions are merely reinforcing we are unable to feel or we shouldn't have to. It is this false belief that keeps them cycling. You are an infinite source of energy, unlimited Love. If you truly believe you cannot feel pain or hurt, that it will kill you, you will never survive. Until you test drive this idea you will never know. You may not even wish to believe you are an infinite source of energy, unlimited Love. I am not really interested in your resistance, just your willingness to choose again, decide for a better way.

When you are anchored in true beliefs and principles you will access deeper clarity and productivity, inspiration and creativity, you can open to these resources because they are a part of you. Our false principles are highly tuned into our five senses, we use them to make decisions about everything and for the most part never ever get to feel the deep intimacy and connection of being anchored in true beliefs. Your true principles become your guide, your light in the darkness. When you feel shut down, afraid, angry, hurt, you get to turn to them for guidance. Your belief in them is your willingness to see your life differently and open up to a new destiny.

Anchoring in false principles perpetuates loveless thinking, making you most vulnerable to choose badly. You know what I mean when you say things you don't really mean and do things you regret. Our beliefs here are false and will always lead us astray. There is no connectivity here, no intimacy with your own heart. There is no permanent peace here, no permanent deep rest, even though within you all of these levels exist. Here temporary peace, temporary rest, temporary happiness all depend on what you believe is outside of

PRINCIPLE THREE

you. Controlling others, our lives and striving relentlessly to achieve this level of mind is impossible.

※

Just as there are no monsters under the bed of our small child to conquer, there is nothing you are up against, it is simply a shift a shift of power you make when you see the misunderstandings you once believed. This is a moment to moment adventure. However, until we see how we are moving and pointing our inner compass and thus our power, we will always believe our choices and our life are subject to an external power. To wake up is to own your life and to want above all else to disassemble every belief that holds you bound to the machine, and all that it represents in your life. It is like an unhappy child that has learnt to bully others to fulfil its own needs, remember the bully and the victim are trying to fix the same dilemma. So before we look without and want to begin creating a better life, a better version of ourselves, and fulfil our dreams it would seem our only real choice is to look within and begin together to draw out the monsters we have created and put them to rest forever. Beliefs are all that binds us to what we fear. What can you have that you do not have already? What can you become that you are not already? What can you be given that you do not already possess? Material possessions are not able to fulfil our hearts and souls, even the most impoverished person can find the gold within and embrace the greatest gift a human being can ever possess, the purity of their own true nature. The great news is that there are no internal villains you need to conquer or destroy. This is only a story that exists in the surface levels of our minds. False beliefs become false principles, as you anchor yourself here you divide your mind and seek safety. In reality we will only find true safety in the knowledge of our true nature.

As you begin to open your eyes, slowly at first and notice how much time you spend bound to this level of thought, you begin to see your thoughts that arise every microsecond are similar. They say the same things, draw the same conclusions, repetitive to the core and even if they sound different now and again they are always needing and wanting something to find true happiness. They are our greatest addiction as a species and yet we don't have AA meetings for this addiction yet. We instead separate this addiction into categories; alcoholism, drug addiction, sex addiction, depression, anorexia, bulimia, self-harming, obsessive-compulsive disorder.

The part of you that has accepted false beliefs and principles believes to feel hurt and pain will literally kill you, it will not survive a broken heart. Think of a love song that repeats this chorus. You know the ones. When we want to believe what is false we move falsely, and in reality, this is so peculiar it is completely foreign to reality. When we are afraid of feeling hurt or pain we are always moving away from it, trying to control the uncontrollable and often feeling very helpless because of this. Regardless of what we feel, we are always turning away from our own heart. We know deep within our own minds we are fooling ourselves. So we want to move away from pain and towards pleasure. You might say,

PRINCIPLE THREE

what is wrong with that? Let's take a closer look, be brave because right about now you may feel all manner of feelings, work with me here and let us untie the shackles around your wrists and your ankles together.

A small immature mind built this mess, let's take it down and rebuild it.

Why? Because it limits you beyond your wildest imaginings and hurts you. Even when we depress, we experience an odd sense of satisfaction as we prove our false beliefs are true. For example, nobody loves me, I am a failure, these two will do for now. These false and devastating beliefs bind us to a life sadly lived. How can you choose these beliefs and feelings that were decided upon by a small child who has been running your Love life and doing a terrible job? You are not bad because you depress and feel some satisfaction, it is how the mechanism keeps turning. The moment you look at this without feeling judged by someone, like me, for example, who truly sees you, yes that's right I love you and I don't even need to know you because I too, was like you, confused filled with misunderstandings and false beliefs, until I woke up. I am not an enemy, I am not trying to make you feel bad or not consider your feelings. I am here to tell you, you are amazing and filled with extraordinary potential. You just need to decide if depressing or angering and believing false thoughts still serves you or if you are ready to light up the room.

We are not able to decide against our own beliefs when they remain hidden from us, this is why we can use our life to uncover these immature beliefs and gently release the need for them. Recently a dear person in my life had to make an important decision. He was pondering and trying to figure it out. With a part of him being pulled by his hidden beliefs and part of him seeing an opportunity opening, he was in a conundrum. Conflict always begins within our minds, hidden beliefs pulling us in the same old direction, the same voices feeding us the fear and the justification for why we should take a certain action. If we don't question we will never have a true choice to create our new life. I asked him if he would pass this decision across to the three-year-old within, the part of his mind still immature and unexamined, or would he use the mature part of his mind to decide? It is a valid question. The immature part of you believes in fear, the fear of being hurt, feeling pain it will never survive. It believes in the idea of separation. Would you trust this part of you with the most important decisions in your life? It was an interesting question, without it the past would simply continue to play out in his life. The outcome is unknown and yet a seed has been planted and new realisations are now possible.

It doesn't matter about outcomes, what matters is whether you choose what is true or what is false. This matters profoundly. You will either be here to open your heart or to close it. The small immature part of your mind will always want to close, it's anchored in fear, you are truly needed here to parent this inner child and choose again, only because you can. Your life is meaningful, has deep purpose. Use it rightfully and you will naturally need to use fear less and less, until one day you see how truly meaningless it is.

PRINCIPLE FOUR

False Principle
What is happening right now is wrong.

True Principle
Reality only ever occurs in one way and
it can't be wrong.

Every second that you are here you are unfolding. Your beliefs unfold before you and you have one incredible choice. How will you be with each unfoldment? One hundred percent of the time reality moves according to plan, yet we make it wrong, believing somehow that our universe has unfolded incorrectly. This is impossible. This is so hard to take when life unfolds in ways that are unthinkable, with so many losses and so much pain. However, it is when we resist these experiences however difficult they may be that we suffer deeply. When we deny and resist the unfoldment of reality we are at war. We are at war with reality and therefore we have no peace. In this chapter, I so wish for you to see there are only ever two choices. One may break your heart but you will rise, the other will distort your mind and your heart and leave you at the mercy of negative energies and of course, this includes fear.

> **Open or close.**
> **Soften or harden.**
> **We have a choice.**
> **Everything else is imagination.**

What do I mean when I say you are at war? All war begins within our minds and hearts. We fear war in its physical form; however, this would be impossible if we ended all violence within. When you deny reality as it unfolds and decide to create your own, you are in defiance of the one that is unfolding, this is how you choose war over peace. To defy is to be against something, someone, in this you alone begin your own inner war.

Our thoughts determine the world that we see. Thoughts of gratitude for the smallest of things, for example, open our hearts allowing us to experience our life even for a moment with joy and love. Fearful thoughts have us experiencing the world as fearful and dangerous. Thoughts are powerful and our beliefs even more so.

PRINCIPLE FOUR

The war within is the only war you need to begin to notice and this war can only begin when you are turning your back on reality and suggesting for a microsecond that its unfoldment is wrong. Death is painful, it is not wrong; tragedy is heartbreaking, it is not wrong.

What is most powerful here is your recognition of the lie you once told yourself. It isn't reality that causes us to suffer but instead our own relationship to the lie we once told ourselves and believed. Why, you may ask, would I do such a thing to myself? I am not a liar, I am a good person. I agree with you, we all are made of the same essence of goodness and Love, yet we cannot deny our suffering, our anxiety and our fear. These emotions have risen from our own hand and the hands of our ancestors. Is it not time to release the lie and lean into Love? I am not suggesting this is easy, however, it is so exquisitely simple.

Reality dishes out all of our internal beliefs to us. It isn't our fault when things happen, in fact, they offer us another chance to forgive, to open, to release our pain, the pain we once blocked in the hope of not feeling powerless and helpless. Reality moves one way and the way is the way home for us all. The universe isn't working for you or against you, it is simply unfolding according to your inner beliefs, what you believe you will experience; and when you do, if you are living a lie you will continue to close, to harden and to blame life and others for your circumstances, you will suffer. This endless cycle of powerlessness and victimisation of yourself will continue and no pharmaceutical or recreational drug, relationship, success, food or alcohol will offer you the solution. There is only one solution and it is you. You may not believe this right now but it is the truth. Only the inner lies you feed yourself daily are the misunderstanding.

Let me offer you a beautiful and clear example. Two families suffer the unthinkable loss of a child, the culprit is found and possibly punished. One family experiences the deep grief, unthinkable heartbreak, feels it all and ultimately rises up to live another day. They may have to reach out for help from professionals, learn how to be with deep loss and anger and ultimately pain. The other family reacts differently, they stop at anger and the grief is never truly felt. Anger envelopes them and their lives become a deeper tragedy. They become obsessed with the culprit and hate and vengeance is all they can think of to dull the pain. Each family had the same experience and each chose differently. Their destiny is a testament of their choice. I have not suffered the loss of a child and am deeply grateful for this. I did suffer the loss of a dear brother in tragic circumstances. I experienced the consequences of hate, blame and anger in my mother and even though it was understandable and my heart now goes out to her, her suffering was deeply saddening. It also played out in devastating ways in my life. We are not alone, we are all so connected and it is with my heart truly open that I ask you, what do you want for your life and the lives of your loved ones?

Each of us holds the key to ending war on this planet but first, we must begin by accepting our ability to feel. What this means is that our fear of pain and belief that we can overcome it by taking control of reality, which is impossible, is

We begin to see how we move in our secret inner world, our relationship to our thoughts being the first freedom within.

the place to start looking. Under all of your emotions, there is one feeling – pain. Your resistance, denial, war with pain is a misunderstanding because you possess the ability to feel. When you are in resistance of this universal fact you suffer. Pain is the doorway back into your own heart, you do not need to overcome it or deny it, just FEEL it. Let us explore the idea of depressing for a moment. I use this condition as a verb on purpose, because believe it or not you are choosing to depress, just like you choose to anger, in fact, these two emotions are very deeply linked. The Western world is overcome by this idea of mental illness, chemical imbalances in our brains, all of it feeding the idea that we have no power, no control over how we feel. Finally, we have found something to blame, our brain. Pharmaceutical companies revel in this perspective and feed us the solution, earning billions upon billions of dollars each year. Because we have adopted this perspective, it keeps us from power shifting, by the way when we adopt it as our own belief they are feeding, giving us more and more reasons why it is true. Reinforcement of belief is imperative, we will see reasons to continue believing, the world we see will reflect back to us every imaginable reason why depressing is justified. Are you beginning to see the insanity of this perspective? You believe and therefore you see. You will always, always see the world as you believe it to be. Are you loving the world you see, are you in love with the beauty you find in the smallest things, is your life filled with purpose and meaning like a small innocent child? If not, the world doesn't need to change, you do. If this isn't a powerful thought that resonates in you, look deeper, consider that the world you see is a

PRINCIPLE FOUR

self-fulfilling prophecy. Is your purpose to read the newspaper, watch the daily news, read trashy magazines and feel the horror they feed you? Have you ever asked yourself how many stories in the daily news are about good that has occurred in the world? Why not? Because devastation, horror and terror sell stories, they feed our fear and the big guys know this. Are you aware of how many great, inspiring and wondrous things occur on this planet every day? Why don't they report them, why do we only get given two percent of this wonder? Because the ratings would go down. Drama has a purpose, it feeds and reinforces our own inner environment. Do you want to know why I never read the newspaper or watch the daily news? I am not interested. I trust if there is something I need to know about it will find me. Filling my mind with the pointless negativity and political bullying that occurs on this planet each day is just not my business. My business is to offer my complete attention to power shifting every day. My inner environment, my inner world holds the key to my destiny, not the daily news stories journalists are told to find to inform me. Do your children wake up to the daily news each day, is that the reality you wish to feed them, without even a moment of investigation? Wow! Think about this for a moment. If you have yet to investigate what others are saying to your child, the truth of it, why would you offer it to them? If you believe for one moment that you can trust a newsreader because you like them, trust a station because it's your favourite, you are naïve. Is the daily news fuelling the fear in your mind and heart, leaving you to experience a sense of melancholy and helplessness, even terror at times? Offer yourself some relief and deliberately choose what you watch and read. Set an intention that is for your highest good.

We experience a helplessness to create external change or internal for that matter, which is, of course, impossible without the right knowledge, and this helplessness elicits anger. We get angry and this emotion builds up in our inner world, our physical bodies react with chemical warfare, our stress hormones fire up and our entire state changes. We never consider for a moment that angering holds little value; in fact, we believe anger as an emotion has power and can help us to win the war, it becomes our ally. Remember the war we are fighting isn't real, except within our minds, yet our entire state fuels up and we are in a state of war. War is violent and when it is internal what that actually means is the violence lives on inside us. When anger serves a purpose, it is your way to fight injustice. Rather than feel it you become locked down. Anger never changes anything, in reality, it merely devastates, damages and ultimately leaves you or others feeling helpless and even more powerless. The dullness leads many to depress. Depression is not a thing, but rather an outcome of helplessness, powerlessness, that is linked intrinsically to anger. You might say, 'I am not an angry person, I am depressed.' It almost sounds better. I say you are simply a person who is living a lie you inherited, so would you like to end the lie and live? To the deepest part of your heart, my offering is like a sweet song, I hear you and I know your longing to go home to the Love and innocence you once knew and loved. You can do it once again, I'm here.

PRINCIPLE FOUR

If and when you decide to put true principles into practice in your life, the first thing you will notice is the absence of blame. It will feel uncomfortable at first. As you give up your old ally, you will begin to notice blame no longer holds value. Projecting blame onto others or onto yourself will become irrelevant. As you see that what really matters is you being present in your own life, it brings a new-found inner fulfilment and nurture and you will look forward to choosing to open to reality repeatedly. Your new destiny is before you.

This is an intervention into our own thinking patterns, nothing is wrong right now.

Here on this Earth, there are two realms, one that will show you all that is wrong with the world, you and others, and one that will break your heart and open you up to the deeper parts of Love you never imagined possible.

Let us first look at the difference between suffering and heartbreak. At some point in our lives, we decided both were the same and they are not. The more able we are to feel our feelings, no matter how heartbreaking they may be, the less we will suffer. In fact, we will feel everything and may not suffer at all. Suffering is not natural, it is learned like fear. The voices in our own mind sound like we can't, we are weak or we will break. It's this idea in and of itself that perpetuates the cycle of lack and therefore an absence of fulfilment. Suffering and fear go hand in hand.

The world continues to reinforce this misunderstanding in love songs, feature films, stories. However, despite this being a misunderstanding the whole world seems to live by, we can reverse it and begin the walk back home, together. We can embrace our feelings by not seeing them as enemies, they do not need to be resisted or denied. As mature adults, we can begin the journey to adulthood just like the caterpillar.

To say we can handle the feelings of betrayal, grief, loss and hurt that come up in everyday living is one thing, to prove it to ourselves over and over is the most powerful.

You still believe you need to shut down, you still believe life is wrong when things don't go your way, and you will continue to say what you don't mean to say, and do what you don't mean to do. You will worry needlessly, you will gossip, judge, criticise and blame. These pointless behaviours all come from the core belief that you are weak, not enough. No one anchored in their true identity would ever choose such behaviours. They are simply the game we play when we are living a lie that reality is wrong. You don't have a better way to live. Life's unfoldment, reality's unfoldment is your key to heaven, you may now choose to stop resisting and begin opening your heart to the more that is your true identity.

You must at all costs demonstrate your ability to feel. Your heart cannot be broken, in fact, as you open to sadness, grief, betrayal, loss you will find a wellspring of Love so deep and limitless you will wonder whatever took you so long.

Reality offers us the choice to open or close, soften or harden, everything else is in our imagination, it is a fantasy that hurts. It is a hurt that becomes suffering that never ever need have been.

Everything is perfect just the way it is.

PRINCIPLE FOUR

This intervention into our own built up patterning within is like a heroin addict having his family step in and commit him to a rehabilitation centre. Saying, 'No more hurting yourself'. You don't need your family, you need you, your true identity

When we adopt false principles to live by, it is a little like Newton's Law being completely wrong and yet science is built on it. This is not to say it is, it's merely an example of how the foundation of science itself would be flawed. Without questioning the theories we base our entire belief system on we are at the mercy of bad information, Chinese whispers. Information, when left unquestioned, causes us suffering and a sense of helplessness when the opposite is true.

Even when our beliefs cause us anxiety, fear, even a relentless drive, we rarely look to understand, more often than not we want control. Controlling the external only gives you something to focus on, it offers you a sense of worth and value, even just simply something to do. There is some comfort in the idea that we can control our bodies, our minds, our relationships, our life in general. Honestly, can we? As long as we have something to do and something we still have control of we seem to have some level of happiness. When circumstances occur and we have no control over the outcome we tend to lean into false principles, looking for some reference to use to find solutions. However life doesn't need to be controlled, it needs to be invited in.

True power lies in honesty and openness, in being less amid what is real, not more. Once you truly see this, you will see the value of the path through your own vulnerability.

The Power Shift

Your power lies in your unwavering bravery.

And what is true bravery other than your willingness to be vulnerable? The less you are, the more vulnerable you become. The more you open, the more you are replaced by what is real. In this, you build real ground, honest ground, but such growth, healing and maturity doesn't necessarily feel good. And most probably it will not feel powerful.

Herein lies another key difference between your experience and reality. When you feel angry, when you feel outraged, from within the centre of this anger, not when it's suppressed, but when you're fully embodying it, you feel more powerful. This can cause a foundational misunderstanding of power and what it means to be powerful. It is in this you prove to yourself that you will survive and thus undo all the false beliefs that tell you otherwise.

When you live your life protecting such false ground, you are giving it your reality and holding it in place. In living like this the purpose of your life becomes self-protection. And where there is self-protection, honesty cannot enter, resulting in a world of dishonest fantasies, manoeuvring and manipulating to never be seen. In all of this, we are perpetuating an inner violence. Each choice to self-protect a violent act against reality. We create an enemy that doesn't exist and fear our own weakness, and this misunderstanding keeps us locked out of our own perfect strength, perfect power and perfect Love. We lock ourselves out of our own heart.

We are always at the effect of our beliefs, receiving them consciously and subconsciously.

The Power Shift

If you know the truth of this within you, the healing of such a condition lies in the direct path right through the centre of your own vulnerability. It is only through this path that you will be able to fully realise its falsity. In realising its falsity, you are freed.

When considering power and considering what The Power Shift really is, you must come to realise that your own power is real. Being real it does not have you opposing reality, but rather, fully aligns you with it regardless of your experience. When someone snarls at you with a piercing look, your power does not attack. It is not power but the belief in your own weakness that attacks. Herein lies the key misunderstanding. Closing your heart and contracting within your experience is not a movement toward realising your own power. It is a movement toward locking in its opposite. Your belief in weakness moves to defend, control and attack, because from within such belief, expanding out into your experience are alerts of threat which call for such attack. Your real power does not need defence because your real power is not threatened. It is powerful. In realising this, you open and allow that person's snarl fully in, feeling and embodying your own vulnerability during your experience, while believing your power and moving in your power rather than your weakness. It's through this that you allow the belief in your own weakness to shift. It's through this that you are able to realise your own power.

It's in this you are Power Shifting..

PRINCIPLE FIVE

False Principle
I am trapped by fear and negativity as they have more power than me.

True Principle
Fear and negativity exist only when I give them my power and have them serve a purpose for me.

Power is a centrifugal force of unified connections to codes expelling the movement of belief. What a sequence of words. When this opened up in my mind I had to go looking for answers. What does it mean? I know well and trust the place within me that it came from. I just didn't quite understand it yet.

Every single thought has a purpose, it arises as a temptation or let us say an opportunity. At its very root, every single thought you choose to believe and make real through your belief will define your entire reality. Knowing the truth of this inspires hope. It offers you the mystery and enchantment you may not quite be able to grasp, it calls you to explore the very depths of your own power.

When we are in a car and it takes off at high speed we experience a force and that power pushes us back in our seat. This force, even though we can unequivocally attest to the truth of it in our experience, is not real as proven in the world of physics, it is an illusion. We are only moving forward in reality, even though our experience is that we are being powerfully pushed backward, just like when we are in a car accelerating powerfully forward.

If our goal is to avoid pain and finally fix the problem that caused it, it would mean we are telling ourselves falsely that pain is wrong and bad. The experience of pain via our five senses triggers machine-like reactions. Imagine if a machine has been programmed to switch off automatically when it gets stuck. We switch off and go into reactivity, we fight back, we depress, we gossip, we become dramatic, we create stories and endure them relentlessly, we kill, we hate. Nothing else but the experience of or the want to avoid pain will have us choose our loveless level of our selves faster. We made a beeline for it without question hoping to find some relief, we have become addicted to pain relief and a hunger for pleasure. Our quest

Our inner judge and critic can only have power when it is serving a belief in us.

when we are lost is to look for these feelings or relief from them in false principles. If we turned to our true principles we would see we have all we need to find permanent peace, joy and love. We may even feel useless at first and as though we are not doing something, all we can to fix the situation. We may believe we have to take action, the outcome depends on us.

Is it possible that when we choose to open to the solutions we are longing for they can present themselves? Is it possible our role is to realise we are constantly getting in the way of our own happiness, right now?

This false idea of aversion and attraction is so shallow. It's a misunderstanding. To consider that your life is being decided, your destiny, your dreams built from a space so shallow, loveless and self-serving is a shock at first, and guilt and shame will surface, tempting you to believe in your wickedness and selfishness. You will be challenged to allow such thoughts to rise up and as you notice them, withdraw all of your power.

Thoughts have no power, you do.

When we withdraw our power from what is false, that which has served us for decades in some cases, it is not a small feat, it is a journey. Your life is precious and as you begin to understand the origin of your existence you begin to see the pointlessness of trusting it to what is unsolvable, a puzzle that has missing pieces. To reverse what you have believed and replace this with what is true is a power shift. Your life is all about this reversal of power.

PRINCIPLE FIVE

We begin to see how we move in our secret inner world, our relationship to our thoughts being the first freedom within. We begin to see how thoughts appear and disappear and as we look upon them we begin with love in our hearts to see past them and begin to release the need to make them our own, to choose our identity via their appearance or their lack of appearance. Thoughts arise in our awareness. If we choose to live by them without reflection they will always offer us a relief of some kind, just as a parent would offer a child ice cream if it stopped crying, a candy if it was sad. The relief is necessary because we once again falsely believe we are unable to withstand the pressure of an experience. It is like taking a pill each time we feel a little unwell, our society is accustomed to quick fixes to continue on and to make everything right again. The machine runs and runs and runs and will not stop until the power source is cut off. Pull the source of the machine's power out of the wall and voila, no machine. This doesn't of course mean there is no you. You are not the machine, you are what has been choosing it all this time, now you simply remove the source of power you have fuelled the machine with and offer it to true principles, a higher Love.

To make this idea real, first, you have to have even the slightest willingness to appreciate the possibility that you hold all the power and that you are not a mere mortal with needs and wants but an endless source of infinite power. As you begin to kindly and ever so gently withdraw many of your outdated and false beliefs and begin to embrace the idea that pain is the doorway to your real inner life, your own heart,

False principles are not aligned with universal law. Universal laws are not negotiable.

PRINCIPLE FIVE

your perspective will change, you will open to a new level of curiosity and knowledge. Knowledge that is pure and honest. Pain when fully allowed is indeed the doorway to all the gold nuggets you seek outside of yourself, the Love, the hope, the happiness – allowing it without judgement or fear offers you an unlimited source of Love, compassion, joy and knowledge – it will take you back to your real home.

This remarkable transference of power must be grounded in honesty.

As we begin to give our power to true principles and therefore a true way of being with reality, we experience deeper intimacy, love and joy; we experience more of our true nature and our vision changes. You begin to find within your abilities, what you never imagined; creativity, productivity, clarity and a newfound connectedness to all. True principles will offer you deeper levels of thinking where the heart meets the mind. Where thought is a joy and can bewilder you with its beauty and intelligence. The human being is an infinite source of beauty when true principles prevail.

∞

Last week, I found myself spontaneously thinking about one of my team members, she kept popping into my mind. I knew something was happening for her. She arrived at work and this particular day the sun was shining down and the sky was so blue and clear that it almost seemed invisible. We often have days like this here. As soon as the office door opened I noticed something was different about her. She glided in light and unhindered. Something was definitely different. As the day went on her presence was delightful, she had a new level of clarity and a new level of inspiration for her business and her life, she was on fire. Suddenly her comfort zone had shifted and she was in a new place. As we sat for our daily meeting she began to share what had happened for her during the week. She had experienced a shift, a new clarity and a new level of productivity had opened up within. There was a path within her that had cleared. She mentioned her partner was not in the same place and somehow this brought up frustration for her.

As I listened I became more and more aware of how any shift we have towards what is real for us, as one of my mentors often mentions, is always followed by a pitfall. When we open everything in our familiar self that hasn't caught up, we are with this rising up and it is extremely meaningful. It isn't the clarity and the shift that matters alone, what is most important is our understanding of how to continue this shift within, even when it seems everything from within and without is against it. If this doesn't make sense read it again and again and again. This was a light bulb moment for me in my life and still, often I have the lights go on when I fall back into my familiar self, where guilt, shame, anger, suffering rise up asking for their daily meal. You see, as she felt the excitement for her new clarity she also had an expectation that everyone else should also and if they didn't this brought up fear, leading to frustration.

Her shift was so beautiful, her whole perspective of her life had changed, yet as we mentioned previously our accustomed self isn't done yet. Our conversation later that evening

PRINCIPLE FIVE

was lovely and with her willingness to grow, she opened up some more. This is a small example of how our evolution can be stunted, even when we receive clarity. Let's look at it a little closer. As one level opens with what is new and clear our old patterns are still firmly in place. They haven't been undone. So we have the clear voice and then we have the old voices raging. The more we trust the clear voice the less we will pay attention to what is familiar and old. Even if others in our lives are not agreeing we can gently thank them for sharing and share that we simply don't see it this way. We don't need to fight for our new seeing to be accepted by anyone, not even our own inner dialogue. We must trust our clarity to open up the doors we need for this new seeing to flourish. We need to trust the new over and over until the old literally gives up and subsides. No level of trying to convince others, trying to get them to see or agree, will work. It only confirms how little we still trust what has opened up in us.

As an exercise, if you are triggered by what someone else is saying to you, simply imagine that it is your voice you are hearing. It is never what another says to us that causes us to feel hurt, it is only if we believe what they say that hurt can arise. It's perfect, isn't it?

We have the willingness to experience thought in a completely new way, no matter whether it is a thought in our mind or one that another may share with us. We don't have to believe everything we hear. We choose where our power will go.

Let us look at an ancient idea that many teachers have shared in many different ways. The version I bring you is simple. If when you think of an idea, even if you don't believe it yet, you experience even a murmur, a tiny glimpse of peace or realness, you are heading in the right direction. Right now, anything you believe must be up for enquiry, you cannot possibly take any belief for granted, this is how we stay asleep. Our beliefs will unfold into our life, that is a guarantee, therefore how we are with them will determine which ones we offer our power. Where we place our power is where we place our destiny.

All of our thoughts call on us, they are like visitors in our lives calling for our power. Think of your power as food. What do you want to feed within, your true nature or the insatiable part of you that is anchored in what is false? Power is food for belief and you are the one who chooses. Thoughts do not need to stay and become family unless they are serving a purpose for you. Nothing remains if it is not serving a purpose, not even your beliefs. When it serves a purpose, it has your power and therefore it persists. I am sure you have heard of the self-fulfilling prophecy, think about it for a moment, this is directly related not to your experience but your beliefs. You cannot create real change by changing your behaviour or trying to replace a false belief with a better one. It doesn't truly work like this. Your evolution is deeper than this and far more profound. YOU can change it all. Remember, you choose and the entire universe alters, isn't this truly amazing.

We are always at the effect of our beliefs, receiving them consciously and subconsciously. This is why positive affirmations will not ultimately set you free, but they may help you to navigate your mind towards what feels better and therefore change your experience temporarily. Real freedom is in absolute freedom, it is about re-anchoring, moving your power through the use of true principles. Let's look at it a little closer in the next few paragraphs.

We can spend an entire lifetime trying to change and rearrange the circumstances of our life. If we are doing this, and most of us are, we have a belief that we can one day master our circumstances and finally succeed. Everyone's success on the surface may look different, but deep down we want to be seen, valued, loved.

You are the master of one thing only; your beliefs and what you give your power to. Power has so many connotations in our world, for it is so misused here, but using power honestly is so incredibly innocent and sweet, it is what we can embrace here even in the smallest things. Power is your ally when you see that you are the distributor, the keeper of it. After all, you will be mastered by, bonded to, moment by moment what you give your power to.

You don't master your life, but you do choose which masters do. What does this mean? Are masters outside of you calling for you to choose them? Sounds dramatic but this isn't some sci-fi movie, it is your life and you deserve to know and trust how to walk your true path. Beliefs are masters. When you offer your belief, you are bound by the rules of this belief and you will act accordingly. Is your master one of fear or Love? It is that simple. When you come to see clearly where your real power lies, it offers room for the power shift. When you come to see clearly where your real power lies, you can come to see what real choice is and what real decisions are.

Over time you may come to see that you are not in the management game, you are in the power distribution game. This power lies in your ability to give and withhold energy to and from belief, thereby feeding or starving the forms of meaning that populate your awareness. Any more than this and you will be mastered by illusion.

That is precisely the purpose of illusion, to have you believe you are capable of more, you need to do more, be more, thereby wooing you to hand your power over and be mastered by something that, on its own, has no reality at all. False principles founded on false beliefs need your infinite source of power in order to live. It is you who keeps illusions alive.

You distributing your power forms your own reality, regardless of whether what you are feeling is actually real or not. You are completely empowered to feed illusions or be governed by truth. That is your right as the power-keeper, the keeper of power. You, the power-keeper, get to choose what you will be mastered by and in that you realise your true freedom.

In my personal life, I had a war waging inside of my own mind. I had no idea I was distributing power, I felt like I was at the effect of my life experience and this included all other people. The external world I could see was where all of my power went, I was focused on reshuffling the chess pieces rather than understanding the rules of the game.

To LIVE an authentic life it is necessary to have the ability to find inner peace at any time, no matter what.

The Power Shift

The question, Why did this happen? has long gone for me, I don't spend my time looking for reasons why things are occurring. If I am to know I trust what is far more intelligent will somehow reach me with this, be it in a conversation, a book I read, somehow if the reason matters to my evolution I will be reached. Otherwise, I say let it go and stay focused on your life right now. If the challenge is still surfacing, your answer to it is in this very moment, not what was in the past and especially not why.

When you begin to stop digging for answers to make yourself authentic and real, you will find a deep sigh of relief. You are stepping into a new way of perceiving yourself and the world, you are repositioning your identity away from 'I am flawed' to 'I am whole'. When you do this, you look only for the blocks to love and their removal rather than fixing what you believe to be your identity. You will find endless professionals trying to fix your false identity of yourself. When you stop believing this the direct path to your happiness and true evolution will open. Stop digging and start living, everything you need is here. Remember, our life does not and cannot lie. It is all there for us to see, every brick we have laid that is false that we must remove to know Love.

So, back to my war tattered mind. I think even a more honest appraisal of how I was living was that I didn't know how to live, I was lost and trying. I always believed that I was choosing my experiences, yet the horse had not only already left the stable, it was racing across the paddock and what I was experiencing was the effect of beliefs already moving. When I believed what I was experiencing was either my fault

PRINCIPLE FIVE

or my amazingness, I liked some of my experiences and felt proud and berated myself harshly for others. This is the false principle surfacing once again that I have control and of course gives birth to the inner critic, the inner judge in our minds. If you realised and severed this bond alone by removing all of your power distribution to the inner judge or critic, your life would change and you would be free from one of the most debilitating inner dialogues.

Over time I began to see it wasn't what I had chosen but how I distributed my power. My experience was from a belief that I was bound and the only way to release myself was to change my use of power. If you spend some time exploring and reflecting on this paragraph you may very well experience a complete shift or you may very well resist the idea. Either way is fine as long as you continue to work with it. If you find that you go into resistance, think about what you would lose if you believed in this; what would be the cost to your false identity. You might be surprised.

Our inner judge and critic can only have power when it is serving a belief in us. I was a hard taskmaster on everyone, mostly myself. It was almost as though I had a belief the world owed me peace, love and happiness. I deserved it, rather than I can earn it. You pay and you receive. This is the same with your living, you become aware of a belief. If the belief no longer serves you, you may consider the cost to release it and if you are willing to pay the cost, you will earn the outcome. You pay the costs and you receive, this is like earning the freedom to live authentically. No one owes you happiness, peace or love because honestly, you are the one.

The Power Shift

You are the power-keeper and as you choose to distribute your power you will reap the consequences. However, as we are so externally focused we find this principle so difficult to believe in. We want our experience to be or not be a particular way and we like to believe we have control over the outcomes. We do actually but not when we are focused on the experience, we must see where true power exists and what is moving it.

Let us consider this. Reality only moves one way and yet our experience is completely opposite to this, we feel as though life is coming at us, other energies are entering us. How often have you heard yourself say that someone else's negativity drained you? Within this belief we become enslaved to false principles, leaving us vulnerable and separate from how power really moves and what is moving it. We cannot adopt two principles in the one moment, we are either choosing a false principle or a true one. Many of the principles we live by we have inherited without question or simply adopted. It may now be the time to question your beliefs. Change is often frightening and even if our current way of living isn't fulfilling us, it is better the devil you know than the one you don't. However, in this case, you eliminate the idea of the devil altogether, so what do you have to lose?

We can see now the misuse of power is inevitable when we believe in false beliefs that we have never questioned. Suffering is power moving falsely; pain, when opened, will take you deeper, accessing more of your true strength and many other exquisite abilities; the ability to love even when you are hurt; the ability to see honestly even when you are

PRINCIPLE FIVE

not getting your own way; this is where the rubber meets the road. Herein lie abilities that will astound you and yet you cannot enter falsely, the entrance to your deeper abilities and qualities is inaccessible to anything other than your pure heart. You might ask what gives me access. Honesty, that's it! The releasing of the false and the power shift towards your new true principles.

False principles are not aligned with universal law.

Universal laws are not negotiable.

We cannot break them, we will suffer when we choose against them. To fight the reality of the present moment is not only insanity, it turns into suffering and a feeling of helplessness as though it is you against life or those who appear in it. When all your hopes and dreams are projected on the outside world with the hope that one day, somehow all will fall into place for you and if you have been good, determined, goal driven, you may get to be happy for a time, successful even rich, you are living a lie. The way back to Love, inclusion and true connections begins with a simple reversal of principles. Let's test drive this story, experiencing once again one of the true and foundational principles.

I had worked all day in our home office and Toby was working about ten minutes away in our head office. This particular evening I was cooking a new recipe as we had just begun The Plant Paradox diet by Dr Gundry, so it was okra in the oven. I was hungry and had it in my mind that Toby and I would eat together, which isn't always how it works out in

The Power Shift

our household. I had spoken to Toby about an hour earlier and was expecting him to walk through the door any minute. I suddenly got a phone call that he had just left the office. I noticed I felt annoyed and wanted to get off the phone fast. We had had many conversations about when marked the end of our business day and Toby was never really great at keeping set times, he really is his own man and I love him for this. Regardless, this issue was unresolved for me and my mind began to wander. My thoughts seemed harmless yet I noticed I was annoyed. I was thinking about what I would say to him to be sure he knew this wasn't okay. Wow! There it was, my happiness, my peace, my power about to be given. I saw myself opening the door and saying exactly that.Nowadays this sort of reaction is rare. Nowadays, I choose wisely, I know the folly of wanting to be right rather than being loving.

Life offers us incredible gifts when we power shift.

Let us remember, the true principles of the universe are not vague, our return to them is a promise of unbelievable beauty. We have nothing to lose but our false beliefs and the reality they build which leads us to suffering and at times temporary stability. We can lay down our sword and offer our power, moment by moment when we remember honesty, which we can now bring into our lives through our true principles. We will unlearn the false and once again realise our choice to choose reality over fear, love over hate. We can begin our journey back home where the mystery of what we are will unfold. Reality always moves one way and this way is forward.

PRINCIPLE FIVE

In physical form, you are moving energy, or so it seems, yet if you didn't have even one belief, nothing to move toward, you would simply be Love. Love moving. Therefore what we need to consider is the power and purpose of belief.

In our society we believe to be empowered is to push forward, to never give up. We teach this first to our children through our own reactions, words, body language and then of course through our daily interactions with them and others. We demonstrate what we believe and sadly they project this back to us as toddlers, teenagers and sometimes even as adults. Of course, they then continue to do the same and project the same misuse of power to their children and the cycle continues, however it can end now.

This isn't a game, this is the universe at work and you either live by false principles or true principles. If you choose the false movement of your power you will experience the outcome of this, while if you choose the true you will inevitably experience a different outcome. Let us consider that your son is suspended from school. You ask, 'What do I want the outcome to be?'. This small intervention is the first step as you begin to see that you have choice here. If you choose wisely you would want to support him to rise above his difficulties without the use of guilt, shame and blame. You will be curious and want nothing more than to offer him a kind and loving space to express himself without judgement. You may implement all five principles here, showing him rather than telling him how to deal with what he is feeling. Children and young adults want the adults in their lives to set the terms for their relating. If you choose anger and shame you will reap the consequences.

The Power Shift

Let me offer you a real-life story. This particular morning, life offered me a golden nugget, an opportunity. My daughter was a free spirit and she was to me as I was to her the perfect teacher. She came into the kitchen where my partner and I were cooking breakfast. She was in a foul mood. Teenage style. Everything was a problem, especially me. I could see she was angry, if not in an unhealthy way. Even when we need connection we can step into the ego thought system, let's connect through fighting! I decided this morning not to react to her frequent comments about the smelly food, lack of food in the fridge. Each time I simply repeated inwardly, I choose peace instead of this, a quote I had read from a book I love, A Course in Miracles. This quote just happened to enter my mind this morning. I knew the goodness of it and each time she made a nasty comment, I repeated it. I had taken my attention off her and was minding my own business, what was going on in me, I was power shifting. My intent was to choose peace within, I ignored whatever reactions were arising within me and replaced with the words, I choose peace instead of this. This is an important distinction. I wasn't concerned about my daughter's peace, only by being totally responsible about my own internal choice was I able to demonstrate to her another way. A way of connecting that did not need a fight. I felt an incredible peace and calmness within and began to feel such a deep love for her. Finally, she hit me with, 'You are the worst mother in the world.' She needed to bring out the big guns, to try one last time to see if I would react. Deep within we all

PRINCIPLE FIVE

want deep and profound connections. When we hold the space for each other in these times we are the guardians of Love. I heard a gentle, sweet voice ringing in my ears and replied, 'Thank you for sharing, I don't see myself this way.'

There was a deep quiet in our small but functional kitchen, with the sun streaming outside and the distant sound of the morning train. I sat down. In moments, she came to me and wrapped her arms around me and said, 'Mum, I love you.'

I felt a deep thank you in her words.

I responded, 'I love you too, darling.'

Children respond and recognise love effortlessly. If we do not show them how they can so easily forget and become lost. In this case, my daughter was found. As her mother, I was willing to show her rather than tell her. If I believed that children should listen to their parents, that morning could have been a disaster (and we've had enough of those!). So a miracle was experienced, a confirmation that Love is extended and not expected. Respect, dignity, kindness are all qualities of Love and we get to extend them to others even when they are being hurtful and angry towards us.

This was Love not relating to fear; she didn't want to fight, in fact, if she had asked herself that morning what she really wanted if she was honest it would have been to love. My use of power was internal, I used my power to choose peace over anger and judgement, she loved me for my honest choice. This was a life-changing day. What I also learned was that my choice was not about the outcome, I truly had no agenda, the miracle unfolded naturally as a response to my inner movement of power.

The Power Shift

When you choose the false you will experience unhappiness, stress and most importantly a limited experience. As the infinite source of energy that you are you can choose, this is the outstanding opportunity we have here on this planet, we only need to reclaim it. When you choose false principles, you will feel anxious at times and always be at the beck and call of your negativity and fear. Not because they exist but simply because you are bound to the principles that feed them. Choosing these negative energies is problematic and will make your life a maze of false turns and false ideas. You see the universe has laws that protect us and laws that support our evolution as a human species. We are offered gifts moment to moment as we give our power to the laws of the universe and therefore principles that move in a way that is of benefit. Giving our power to false principles that are a block to love and happiness in the hope that we will have happiness, peace and love in our lives is where all suffering comes from. Giving our power to false principles is like moving our power away from the Love, connection, peace and happiness that we long for. Our true purpose here becomes a mere buried idea that we have forgotten. We cannot find anything permanent when we give our power to what is false and even tiny moments of happiness will be fleeting; one moment we will feel powerful and the next helpless, always needing a crutch to find fulfilment. We will believe in our experiences and put our attention on them and the world outside of us. We will externalise our power and project it onto our life and other people. All the while attempting to survive, cope, be happy or not.

PRINCIPLE FIVE

Happiness is a choice, it has to be learned. Deep within we know how to be happy; however, if we are suffering we have forgotten.

Real giving, giving with no agenda, is your power being given to true principles, rather than to illusion, that's why it feels so good. Real giving is offering your power to reality as it is. For most of us, this is a challenging paragraph. Real giving isn't only about giving to others when we feel good, it is a true and complete opening to reality as it is. Always moving forward openly no matter what.

Your power is your one most profound gift on this Earth, you carry the gifts to move power, always.

We learn early on that thoughts have power, it has been said they can control us and some are good and some are very, very bad. We should fear them and whatever we fear we want to control. We want to change them, be rid of them, replace them. When our thoughts are out of control we feel agitated and unable to relax, this causes us anxiety and if only we could stop our thoughts everything would be okay. We feel powerless and weak, believe our thoughts are more powerful than we are. Miracles unfold naturally as a response to your inner movement of power.

To LIVE an authentic life it is necessary to have the ability to find inner peace at any time, no matter what. Happiness is a by-product of this and without the correct principles, codes or laws you are lost in a matrix. The power of belief is mind altering and in the next few paragraphs, I will share with you one of many miracles I have experienced. I call it a miracle because it was an act of Love. All acts of love that come from our true nature are miracles, they are not reserved for good people with good karma, as you believe, they are there when you choose to give your power to your true nature. When I had my first awakening I was showered with what I called miracles, reality and I were one. I was amazed in one way but in another, I began to see how what was deeper had a different way of moving in this world and I didn't need to be in control but rather I needed to trust it. I learned how to be with reality without resisting it, allowing it even when it hurt to tenderly unfold. When you through trust give it permission to lead the way it will astound you, shower you with gifts.

It was around 1999 when I was working with women, supporting them as they dealt with deep issues in their lives and I had been approached by an acquaintance to see if I could babysit a young foster child she was looking after. She had something come up and couldn't take care of him, his mother a prostitute, a drug addict who needed help. I had two children of my own and was a single mother at the time, and I wondered how I could be of real help, so I turned her down and asked her instead to send me the child's mother. She said she would ask her and see if she was willing to come and have a session with me. I soon found myself in a session with a young woman who was visibly shaking, a little worse for wear and still willing to come and sit with me. I thought at the time what a miracle that was in itself. I promised myself quietly I would only spend an hour with her and not pro-

PRINCIPLE FIVE

long the session. As always, I began to release control of the space and move myself aside, I had developed such trust in the deeper intelligence within, I knew the power of Love, all my sessions were handed over in this way. With a deep relaxation, I allowed myself to surrender to an inner stillness within and hand over to Love.

The young woman began to share her troubles with me, her life story, her pain, her sorrow. Love openly listened, I had no thoughts arise during this time so I didn't say a word. In listening, I noticed we connected deeply. I began to feel her. There was no sympathy for her plight or judgement of her decisions, deep listening is a natural ability we all have when we seek it. Almost forty-five minutes into the session a quiet thought appeared in my awareness, it went exactly like this: Whoever told you, you were bad? I knew to share this with her so I spoke the words and there was silence. All of this so uneventful, just reality unfolding in a moment where Love entered and took care of a human being as only Love can.

As the session came to an end, she offered me an envelope, as I had suggested with a small donation. I think it was $5. I wasn't helping her for money, but I thought some exchange was important. Regardless, the agreement was to offer a donation of what she could afford. Simone left and was on her way, she knew she was welcome to come again if she needed to.

Four days later I received a phone call from her and she said she wanted to come and sing me some songs that she wrote. Of course, I agreed, I was happy to hear from her and noticed she sounded different. When Simone came to my home for the second time she was a completely different young woman, cleaned up, not shaking at all and happy. She told me that she had stopped taking drugs and had left her job at the bar. Her songs were beautiful and she had become yet another miracle in my reality. She continued to visit me for sessions bringing along her donations in an envelope, $5, sometimes $10, and we continued to unravel what was false in her.

Simone found her true nature this particular day, she went on to university and studied psychology, removed her son from foster care and called me every year to wish me a Merry Christmas. Miracles unfold when true principles replace the false and I've experienced this with Simone and many others. You choose always, you choose every part of your experience here. The challenging part for us to accept is that the choices we have made, buried deep within our own subconscious, have us feel as though we are victims, and not actually the architect of our own experience.

As the power-keeper, you have all the power. Even though more often than not you experience a sense of powerlessness, even helplessness, this only occurs because of your anchoring during this time in false principles. You see there may be times you feel powerless and helpless but if you open to these feelings you will see they are just energy moving and have no story attached to them.

You are never powerless or helpless.

I spent decades using my feelings to tell me what was true and where to give my power and it was a sad day when I realised how much of my life I had wasted playing out this

PRINCIPLE FIVE

misunderstanding. As you begin to practise power shifting, you will find undeniable beauty and your life will bloom of your own making.

The Power Shift means you choose where to distribute your power and the reason for this is simple, bad habits repeated many times become patterns, patterns become embedded in our nervous system. Your reactions happen so instantly you feel completely helpless to take control. It is as though you are powerless. Belief moves at the speed of lightning before you even have an opportunity to think, therefore you feel as though you have not chosen. The opposite, of course, is true.

The belief you once upon a time inherited in your life remains to be seen now. This is the unique opportunity life offers us when our reactions lead us to the beliefs lurking within. Let's go back for a moment to the powerlessness we feel, we shan't ignore this, we must relate to this reactivity in a new way, otherwise, we will be trapped and not know how to undo it. Here is where we bring in the exquisite tools of kindness and forgiveness. In reality, there is nothing to forgive as you step into your true nature, the past does not exist and nor does the future, only what you are choosing now is meaningful. However, it is a sweet and beautiful idea and we will use it to offer you everything possible to make the shift.

Consider this common scenario for most parents. Your child has hit their sister and made her cry and your reaction to your child most commonly would be to raise your voice and even punish them. As you raised your voice you could see the fear in their eyes, and a part of you was satisfied, they deserved it, as you looked upon his sister sobbing in the corner. If you stay with the 'they deserved it' part of this scenario, you will probably not be ready to reflect on your reaction. This is not to say you can prevent thought, but you do not need to believe it. We are all learning here and punishment and fear are very bad teachers. In this moment, your reaction seemed to happen without you being able to control it. This is going to happen often as you have made inroads in your nervous system. As one of my favourite texts states, the horse has already bolted. You see it isn't about the reaction anymore, it is very much about whether you will react or respond to the reaction. Let me spell it out. You can dive right into feeling bad and judging yourself for your failure to be a perfect person or you can notice what was once normal to you is now outdated and even though it presents itself in your life, it no longer serves you. From this kindness, you may apologise to your child for losing your temper, letting them know how sorry you are that you frightened them. Then you can deal in a mature and wise way with their choice to hit their sister. Remember, a tooth for a tooth, an eye for an eye is a false belief. This false belief (lie) creates an endless cycle of violence within and when we are invested in this false belief the world will reflect violence and terror also. What matters most is what is happening within. Everything is within you, if you don't find love in it, change it. This is where true salvation lies.

If we are to look at how power works we can use another example I hear often when I am connecting with my business colleagues, one that has had a powerful impact on my life. With so much now available to us we find ourselves always grasping for more. More success, better careers, more children, more money, more houses, more clothes, more pleasure, more vacations, more, more and more. What an exciting world we live in, filled with opportunity and yet we probably are facing the highest stress levels ever recorded in history, except for when a country is at war. Drug companies are having a field day playing on the idea that our brains are chemically out of balance and need their drugs, our children are faced with new mental conditions and they need drugs too, we plague ourselves with tasks, keeping up with our own relentless expectations. I am not going to even tell you that you are asking too much of yourself, that is for you to decide. However, if you are stressed, unhappy and the most important relationships in your life are suffering, you might need to rethink your goals and your expectations. First, begin by writing them down and then ask yourself what is your end goal? Overwhelm is a label for the way we deal with intensity and pressure. We feel as though everything we need to complete, take care of in our world is pushing on us. We feel trapped and unable to fulfil all our promises to ourselves and others. We have learned to contract under pressure, making this feeling even more intense. By using true principles you will be amazed what you are capable of, minus stress. You will be the realisation of a mature person with real solid ground within aiming for the stars. You will know when you are being true or if you are asking too much of yourself and you will be gentle and kind in the times when you need it the most. Stress is debilitating and causes illness, it is instigated by false principles. As you begin to bring a new awareness to your daily life opportunities will present themselves endlessly. There is no lack of learning and with sincere practice, you will begin to notice the change in you. You will experience unexplained moments of joy and happiness, for no reason whatsoever. You may find yourself interested in creative endeavours, after all, you will have more energy and more power to move in productive and wondrous ways.

The identity built on false principles has its own language. One of its strongest beliefs is that your power can be withheld or can be projected outwardly onto others. As you begin to use true principles you will see it only as a smoky haze which you can move through without even a thought arising. There is really nothing to be done with what is false except to withdraw your belief in what it promises. Your need to engage with what is false over time will become less and less and in its place, you will find the beauty of a real and authentic life.

No matter where you look in this world you will find the perfect training ground for the misuse of power. In our early life, we learn from those around us and from our own choices how to misuse our power and be unhappy. Therefore if we know we have learned how to be unhappy through the misuse of our power we are left with only one clear choice, let us learn how to use it authentically.

Everything has to be practised repeatedly to be done well. This is the same for happiness. When you begin undoing a false way of using power and replacing it with a true principle, it may very well become your life's work. If this is all you do here for the rest of your life you will have a life well spent.

PRINCIPLE FIVE

True power doesn't need force, it has nothing to get and nothing it needs. Your true power is spontaneous and you have the privilege of moving it constantly. You are after all the power-keeper who has an entire bagful of beliefs, some you are aware of and others that lie buried in your subconscious, your only access to them in how your life repeats itself, over and over again. It became clear to me that all I needed to learn I already had in my life, showing me the way, even when I thought I knew better. I also knew my life didn't lie.

The first and honest use of power is to move you to what is most open and dear. This offers us the opportunity to move what we cannot see but know the goodness of. When we see a small child, a baby and look into its eyes our only thought is to love, the baby will give all of its power to you, both of you meeting in Love. Power used to impact the lives of others purely for the sake of goodness is uncommon in our world. We have been trained that to have more is to be more powerful, to stand up and not be dominated is to be powerful, that power is something to acquire rather than to use to move the most precious essence of the universe, Love. We even believe Love is weak and anger is powerful. How wrong we are.

Wherever you put your power your life will go. Even a man in a cell with four walls can uncover the mystery of the power shift. The power shift isn't reserved for the wealthy, the successful, in fact, if we don't begin teaching it in our school system we will forever live limited and unfulfilling lives no matter what shiny objects we dangle before our next bit of fulfilment. A human being who is fulfilled inwardly can still have shiny objects, she would know which ones are of value and which ones are not. She would be discerning and her thoughts would lean more into giving than taking. The shiny objects are fine yet they are second to what must come first, otherwise, we are left craving, chasing these shiny objects for our time in the hope of one day being fulfilled.

A friend and colleague recently said to me, 'I am open and want feedback while I am growing up.' Wow, what a beautiful statement. Mind you, this woman is in her forties and very grown up, but what she is alluding to is growing up in her own thinking, feeling, emotional body. She is saying yes to her first parenting, that of herself. With growing up comes growing pains and sadly these growing pains stop us from using our life for its highest purpose, yet it does not need to be this way. Protecting ourselves from our growing pains is like saying to a child who is experiencing physical growing pains that pain is wrong, they should not grow, this shouldn't be happening. We would never do that, it is part of a child's journey to go through this painful experience. As kind and loving parents, we explain to the child what is happening to its physical body and support it as it opens to the pain. If a child closes it suffers, if it opens it learns its inner strength to deal with pain and becomes resilient and fears pain less and less. When a child learns how to be with physical pain it has a great chance to explore emotional pain and how it can be with it, without closing its heart and mind, without hardening and shutting down.

To reclaim our power as women, we went through a feminist movement, looking upon men as our oppressors

PRINCIPLE FIVE

and projecting our own sense of worth and value outside of ourselves. Our false selves needed to do something to finally be seen and valued. We needed to protest and to seek validation from the world and others, and still millions of women believe they are not equal to men. This is the only place you can believe in the idea of inequality. This is the first correction that must be made in your minds before you can bring change into the world. Otherwise, you contort yourselves and your actions, even though they may create some change, will have a very high price tag and will separate you from what you love the most, to feel connected and one with all creatures and beings you see in your world.

This does not mean activities to change things in the world are meaningless, equal pay and equal opportunity are important, nevertheless, real change begins from within first.

Success, equality does not begin in the eyes of the other, we are not children anymore who looked upon our parents and hoped that one day they would see our worth. We are not teenagers who need the respect of our peers so we can feel lovable and worthy. These are all false beliefs and when left unquestioned they remain in our subconscious and whether we know it or not they constantly have us seeking validation. Even for those who will scoff at this idea, my challenge to you is to look at your life and be honest. For some the beliefs, we harbour are covered in a far more sophisticated way, we have many masks to hide our inner fears and false beliefs, none of them worth keeping.

I often have the honour of speaking to women who are in the midst of or even at the precipice of their dreams. One thing is for certain, success isn't about one part of our lives, true success is about our entire life working. All of it. If one part of our life falls apart and we achieve worldly success, what's the point? Our lives fall apart for one reason, for us to open and see, to choose again. If you choose to be driven in the hope of finding what you already have within, you can now decide for honesty, look at your life with an open heart and mind and avoid the consequences of being led by what is false. Your success is in your honesty and power shifting, not in what the world offers or denies you. In this, you will find peace, deep Love and your true destiny. Remember, your life doesn't lie.

Through exposing the erroneous forms of meaning we've given life and solidified our identity in, an opposing idea could actually cancel us out. We're under an attack of meaning and the ground we're standing on isn't stable. This becomes the source of fear. We're experiencing the lack of reality in a part of ourselves and self-preservation kicks in to defend it.

Change can feel terrifying.

We can even label ourselves as a person who doesn't like change, yet change is a part of real living and only when we embrace it does the caterpillar begin its rebirth. We fear change often because we believe it comes with a price and sometimes we think the price is too high. Yet we must ask ourselves, is this really true?

Even though we may think we are able to fool others, are we really able to fool ourselves? When that moment comes that fooling yourself is no longer a rewarding option

PRINCIPLE FIVE

you have hit a huge milestone in your maturity. This has to happen because only then does the willingness to grow as a woman, a person increase.

The most rewarding time of my life thus far was when I worked as a counsellor supporting women suffering from anorexia, bulimia, self-esteem issues and depression. I spent much of my time as a single mother, learning, growing and praying. When I say praying, it wasn't your conventional version of praying, but rather finding my way back to the voice within me that I had begun to trust above all other voices. A gentle, quiet voice that was always there when I chose silence within. I discovered my greatest problems and challenges were best left in its hands. Rather than anguishing over questions I had about anything, business, my life, my children, silence was the place where I always turned. Even if the answers weren't immediate, I had found peace. This was the premise for my work with my clients. I will share with you a case study in which the name has been changed and here we will witness the incredible power of identification.

Jasmine, 37 years old, mother, divorced.

Jasmine contacted me after hearing me interviewed on an Australian national radio station. She reached out and began working with me to change her life. She suffered from pain in her body and depression. When she arrived, we became acquainted and she shared her story with me and I relaxed and listened. I loved my workspace as I opened to deep listening and Love. I had a way of immediately accessing a holy space within. My dedication and surrender to this holy space was absolute in these times.

The Power Shift

I picked up quickly that Jasmine was angry, even though if you asked her she would never admit this, she would say she was depressed and often looked outside of herself for the reasons behind her depression. If she wasn't punishing herself she was projecting her problems on others or the world in general. False principles make us hard and bitter even at the best of times. In listening, I began to sense her anger and beneath this her pain. No one starts out as a bad toddler and we are not bad people, however, we learn bad habits and inherit some heavy patterns at times that when repeated become destructive.

Our session began with Jasmine sharing her story, she began slowly and then gained momentum, showing me how much energy she had invested in her story. She was venting, letting off steam, lifting the lid off the pressure cooker so to speak. This is the purpose of venting, we believe if we can just talk about it we will feel better, release the pressure; however, this is only momentary. Our inner dialogue over time builds up as energy in our system and causes pressure that we think we need to release. This temporary venting and feel good simply reinforces our destructive patterns and is almost like picking up the top of the pressure cooker to let off steam and pressing repeat, over and over again. It is a pattern of pressure release and does not work. It does not create real change ever. However, for Jasmine, in this case, we had to begin somewhere and she had begun to reach out, her willingness to find help was her first step in the right direction. She was a sweet-hearted woman who had picked up some bad habits and felt trapped inside her own life. Her business

Every second that you are here you are unfolding. Your beliefs unfold before you and you have one incredible choice.

was suffering, her potential unrealised, her family and her intimate relationships always unstable and unsatisfying.

Jasmine's parents, like most of us, had no idea how to deal with their own anger. Whether we suppress anger or project it onto others, it's wrong. Think about it for a moment, would asking a tiny toddler's advice on how to use her power be a trustworthy response? This is where Jasmine was, still trapped in a decision she had once made and her present life reflected this in all her relationships, first the relationship with herself and then with the world. If we could rewind and change that one decision in our life as a tiny toddler our lives would very possibly have had a completely different outcome. Same circumstances, different quality of life, maybe even different opportunities, who knows. However there are no rewind buttons, just a wondrous opportunity to choose again.

Jasmine didn't choose to project her anger outwardly on others, she had tried it as most toddlers and learnt early on that her anger meant fear and punishment from the ones she loved in her world. Her early memories were that her tantrums made her mother mad and she would stare her down and even pull at her little arm, just to get her attention, all in the hope of having her stop. A reaction such as this in the eyes of a child is terrifying. Jasmine recalled some of these memories and even her thoughts at the time. In this moment we are offered two paths, fear or Love. Most of us choose fear and fear has a voice all of its own. Once we take it to heart we are bound to it. Jasmine was fortunate enough to want to undo what she had done so many decades ago.

PRINCIPLE FIVE

As a child, Jasmine's power was surging through her and it is natural to require support and help, for a child to be guided when taking this developmental step. However, this is not common as most of the world's parents are yet take this step themselves. Therefore as adults, we are left to undo the old pattern we made up. Jasmine's depression was her inability to deal with her own anger, pain, we could say power, and therefore how to take care of her own wants and needs. Remember, they were the purpose of the pain and anger in the first place. Let's look at what happened a little more closely together.

What struck me as beautiful about this story was that Jasmine was open to accepting she was as a young child, the one who closed her heart, turned away from pain. She was not in denial. She was open to the idea that if she built this mess within her own mind, even what she inherited, then she could now reverse it. This was truly a miraculous moment. She was ready for change, she was looking for a new way.

Jasmine was an amazingly talented woman and yet she never really was able to reach her potential. Her inner life was stunted because her power was misplaced, invested in the false, draining her and leaving her feeling helpless or highly driven. She hadn't built inner stability based on true principles yet!

Jasmine wanted to live a better life, to build beauty and have her day at her disposal rather than at the whim of her emotions and thoughts. She truly wanted more intimate and deep relationships, family bonds that reflected her ability to be Love in the true sense of the word. She wanted it all and she was willing to see, understand and do whatever was necessary. It was this openness to change that was the guiding light to her lying low in her inbuilt cocoon, accepting the choices she had made in her life and with each little piece of honesty releasing the butterfly within.

For Jasmine, no longer giving her power to the destructive patterns she had made was like losing a part of herself. She was so strongly identified with her patterns and they seemed like they made up a part of her, yet with each session, she began to see each of her patterns and their purpose. As she saw the purpose she had made them for in the first place, she was able to decide for a new purpose and create new patterns of goodness and beauty in her mind and heart. As she began to implement true principles into her life she was learning how to live the life she knew was possible, all that was missing were true principles. For Jasmine, the timing was just right and she was ready. Her life changed.

A new destiny awaits you, too.

The reason for looking for more meaning in your life doesn't really matter, all will unravel perfectly in everyone's quest to free themselves of the self-imposed shackles that exist in the mind.

LOGOS (λόγος)

You may be wondering why the word 'logos' (λόγος) appears so often in my book.

This ancient word was first introduced to me as a young girl by my father. He taught us all how to read, write and speak Greek. He was relentless in his quest to have his heritage survive, even as an immigrant, thousands of miles away from his treasured homeland. His children were his way of ensuring it lived on.

Decades later, an astrologer friend of mine, whilst reading my chart, kept alluding to this word "Logos" and how he was seeing it appear all around me. He went on to say he could see women all around me with blank faces, waiting to hear what I had to say. I didn't really understand the deep meaning of this word.

At that time, I was writing fairy stories and I wondered if my books would be published and I would meet women this way. I never once imagined The Power Shift would emerge. When I walked away with Toby, I was quizzical for a day or so and then the thought just faded. I didn't think much of this again until the day I began to look for a symbol to add to The Power Shift; a meaningful symbol.

The word λόγος appeared before me as I began my search for a symbol that would represent The Power Shift. It felt like out of nowhere the word appeared on my iPad - λόγος. You may ask, how does a word appear when you are searching for a symbol - the mystery of life unfolding. I recognized it and felt drawn to it as if it was speaking to me, telling me to look deeper and explore it more. It was calling me in. My exploration took me through many diverse explanations, but first came the Greek philosophical meaning - the divine reason implicit in the cosmos, ordering it and giving it form and meaning.

My heart and my mind immediately led me back to the the 5 True Principles of The Power Shift.

I experienced a powerful humility within, as if I had been brought to my knees; gratitude and brokenness revealing to me the beauty of truth and how it finds us when we are willing to say, "Yes".

As I continued on I found Christology had its own meaning for 'logos' - a name or title of Jesus Christ, the word of

God. Once again I was reminded, holiness exists within each of us and we are invited, moment by moment, to offer our life to it, to lean into it and say "yes"; a "yes" above all else, to purity of heart. It doesn't matter what theology we lean towards, what our heart's desire is or what our faith is. What is most important, however, is that we have the courage to recognize that truth is the same for all of us and faith mustn't divide us, but rather, bring us closer together.

> **"Listening not to me, but to the Logos, it is wise to agree that all things are one."**
> **- Heraclitus**

NOTES

NOTES

NOTES

NOTES

NOTES

NOTES

NOTES

NOTES

www.ingramcontent.com/pod-product-compliance
Lightning Source LLC
Chambersburg PA
CBHW071919290426
44110CB00013B/1414